New Directions for
Higher Education

Betsy O. Barefoot
Jillian L. Kinzie
Co-editors

Issues in Distance Education

Maureen Snow Andrade

EDITOR

Number 173 • Spring 2016
Jossey-Bass
San Francisco

922630744

ISSUES IN DISTANCE EDUCATION
Maureen Snow Andrade
New Directions for Higher Education, no. 173
Betsy O. Barefoot and Jillian L. Kinzie, Co-editors

Microfilm copies of issues and articles are available in 16mm and 35mm, as well as microfiche in 105mm, through University Microfilms Inc., 300 North Zeeb Road, Ann Arbor, MI 48106-1346.

NEW DIRECTIONS FOR HIGHER EDUCATION (ISSN 0271-0560, electronic ISSN 1536-0741) is part of The Jossey-Bass Higher and Adult Education Series and is published quarterly by Wiley Subscription Services, Inc., A Wiley Company, at Jossey-Bass, One Montgomery Street, Suite 1200, San Francisco, CA 94104-4594. POSTMASTER: Send address changes to New Directions for Higher Education, Jossey-Bass, One Montgomery Street, Suite 1200, San Francisco, CA 94104-4594.

New Directions for Higher Education is indexed in Current Index to Journals in Education (ERIC); Higher Education Abstracts.

Individual subscription rate (in USD): $89 per year US/Can/Mex, $113 rest of world; institutional subscription rate: $335 US, $375 Can/Mex, $409 rest of world. Single copy rate: $29. Electronic only–all regions: $89 individual, $335 institutional; Print & Electronic–US: $98 individual, $402 institutional; Print & Electronic–Canada/Mexico: $98 individual, $442 institutional; Print & Electronic–Rest of World: $122 individual, $476 institutional.

Editorial correspondence should be sent to the Co-editor, Betsy O. Barefoot, Gardner Institute, Box 72, Brevard, NC 28712.

Cover design: Wiley
Cover Images: © Lava 4 images | Shutterstock

www.josseybass.com

CONTENTS

EDITOR'S NOTES

In 1960, the United States ranked first in the world for undergraduate degree attainment (Lumina Foundation for Education, 2010). It currently ranks sixth (Lee & Rawls, 2010). Despite this, from 2000 to 2009, undergraduate enrollments rose by 34% (Aud et al., 2011). These figures are projected to grow further as 66% of jobs in the United States will require some form of postsecondary education by 2020 (Carnevale, Smith, & Strohl, 2010). Consequently, governments, educational institutions, and organizations have set goals to increase the percentage of college graduates (Lee & Rawls, 2010; Lumina Foundation for Education, 2013).

One means to increase access and completion is distance learning. This includes offering online degrees to admitted students or coursework to millions of users through open educational resources or massive open online courses (MOOCs). Because of disruptive technological change, institutions must determine the extent to which they will develop and offer online programs, which ones, how many, for whom, and why. They must make decisions about development models, design, processes, costs, and support. Related issues include perceptions of quality, lack of faculty support, and competition with for-profit and online institutions.

Scope and Purpose

Distance learning is playing an increasing role in institutional strategic planning (Allen & Seaman, 2013). Campuses have varying reasons for adopting distance learning such as scheduling flexibility, completion, and space constraints. The purpose of this volume is to guide decision makers as they determine appropriate responses to distance learning opportunities. The volume covers a range of topics appropriate to those developing an initial infrastructure, revitalizing existing structures and processes, or desiring to innovate and lead the field.

Chapter Outline

In Chapter 1, Michael Beaudoin reviews the evolution of distance learning in higher education and identifies three responses—a trend unlikely to have positive or long-lasting effects, an unproven model with questionable

NEW DIRECTIONS FOR HIGHER EDUCATION, no. 173, Spring 2016 © 2016 Wiley Periodicals, Inc.
Published online in Wiley Online Library (wileyonlinelibrary.com) • DOI: 10.1002/he.20174

quality, and an approach with potentially impressive results. Current threats include profit-focused models, resistance, lack of awareness, and fear. Opportunities involve access, growth, innovation, expansion, partnerships, and learning enhancement. Beaudoin conceptualizes distance learning as a disruptive innovation that accounts for resistance and the need for a directed, strategic institutional response. The chapter identifies characteristics and practices for transformative leadership.

Understanding distance education theory is critical to launching and sustaining effective programs. In Chapter 2, Farhad Saba reviews the origins of distance education as a discipline and the development of theories to provide common ground for decision makers. He defines distance education, illustrates its responsiveness to the needs of individual learners, and explains how dialogue, structure, and autonomy (Moore, 2013) can individualize instruction. Related to the concept of disruptive technologies, he urges institutions to adapt and offer flexible educational opportunities to prepare learners for the innovation needed in their future professions. Saba introduces the community of inquiry model to demonstrate how social, cognitive, and teaching presences interact and overlap.

In Chapter 3, Maureen Snow Andrade leads decision makers in considering structural models for distance education at institutional (macro) and project (micro) levels. She analyzes the advantages and disadvantages of various models and poses guiding questions. Innovations include team-based development and community building among stakeholders. She poses four interrelated leadership frameworks for creating and managing change.

Chapter 4 transitions the focus from broad considerations to specific development processes. Karen Franker and Dennis James explain the usefulness of a development plan to ensure course quality and consistency. The plan entails the elements of communication, resources, policy, and technology. Structures and processes from development to delivery to evaluation must be clearly delineated to produce quality programs.

Aubrey Olsen Bronson, in Chapter 5, illustrates the resource-intensive iterative process of online course development. This includes time to plan, build, pilot, revise, and launch. Bronson addresses issues of teamwork and the roles of team members. She explains how technology can support a quality learning experience in terms of embedded course support, instructor dialogue, and quality interaction, providing examples of various course design and instructional strategies. The chapter focuses on the micro level to provide administrators with insights into course development; the roles, responsibilities, interactions, and problem-solving processes of collaborative design teams; and decision making to ensure a quality learning experience.

A critical issue in successful distance learning is faculty and learner support. Faculty may need professional development to increase their skills for course development and teaching. Online learners must be assured of appropriate support, which requires coordination across service units. Sharon Guan and Daniel Stanford explicate these issues in Chapter 6. They

NEW DIRECTIONS FOR HIGHER EDUCATION • DOI: 10.1002/he

indicate approaches for integrating online learning into strategic plans, establishing policies and procedures, incentivizing faculty, centralizing instructional design services, ensuring needed student support, and developing advocates for online learning.

Chapter 7 outlines considerations for global expansion. Maureen Snow Andrade establishes the rationale for global expansion, presents guiding questions, and provides an overview of language acquisition issues that impact the success of online learners who speak English as a second language. She establishes the need for learners to be self-regulated or to possess the ability to control factors that affect their success, and how the development of this ability can be embedded into a course.

Continuing the theme of global distance education, in Chapter 8, Alan Young presents the case study of Brigham Young University–Idaho and the innovative process implemented to expand higher education access to learners who may otherwise be restricted by academic preparation needs, traditional forms of delivery, cost, and even lack of confidence. Young traces the steps in the process from initial development to the current highly successful and growing program. He cites disruptive innovation as a guiding concept (see also Chapter 1) and explicates how leaders managed the organizational change required for stakeholders to adapt and evolve from a traditional model.

Finally, Marjorie Leon and Todd Price conclude the volume in Chapter 9 by examining the effects of disruptive technology on higher education. Beginning with a brief history of technological disruption, the authors explicate its effects on students, faculty, and administrators, and explore deliberate institutional responses such as online programs, open source materials, flipped classrooms, professional development, learning object repositories, and MOOCs. The chapter provides examples of institutions that have implemented these innovations, and cites the results of interviews with stakeholders.

Conclusion

This volume presents a comprehensive view of distance learning in higher education from its beginnings through its evolution as a discipline to its increasing widespread presence on traditional campuses. It presents both macro and micro views of distance learning to provide institutional decision makers with a broad and in-depth understanding of its potential and challenges. The volume establishes the need for effective strategic planning and leadership to develop responsive approaches enabling institutions to embrace disruptive innovations and shape the futures of their faculty and students.

Maureen Snow Andrade
Editor

References

Allen, I. E., & Seaman, J. (2013). *Changing course: Ten years of tracking online education in the United States*. Babson Park, MA: Babson Survey Research Group and Quahog Research Group. Retrieved from http://www.onlinelearningsurvey.com/

Aud, S., Hussar, W., Kena, G., Bianco, K., Frohlich, L., Kemp, J., & Tahan, K. (2011). *The condition of education 2011 (NCES 2011-033). U.S. Department of Education, National Center for Education Statistics*. Washington, DC: U.S. Government Printing Office. Retrieved from http://nces.ed.gov/pubsearch/pubsinfo.asp?pubid=2011033

Carnevale, A. P., Smith, N., & Strohl, J. (2010, June). *Help wanted: Projections of jobs and education requirements through 2018*. Washington, DC: Georgetown University Center on Education and the Workforce. Retrieved from http://cew.georgetown.edu/jobs2018/

Lee, J. M., & Rawls, A. (2010). *The college completion agenda, 2010 progress report. National College Board Advocacy and Policy Center*. Retrieved from http://completionagenda.collegeboard.org/sites/default/files/reports_pdf/Progress_Report_2010.pdf

Lumina Foundation for Education. (2010, September). *A stronger nation through higher education*. Retrieved from http://www.luminafoundation.org/states_landing/a_stronger_nation_through_education/

Lumina Foundation for Education. (2013, June). *A stronger nation through higher education*. Retrieved from http://www.luminafoundation.org/stronger_nation_2013/downloads/pdfs/a-stronger-nation-2013.pdf

Moore, M. G. (2013). The theory of transactional distance. In M. G. Moore (Ed.), *Handbook of distance education* (3rd ed., pp. 66–85). New York: Routledge.

MAUREEN SNOW ANDRADE *is associate vice president of Academic Affairs for Academic Programs at Utah Valley University. Her responsibilities include distance learning, faculty development, assessment, curriculum development, degree completion, general education, and graduate studies.*

NEW DIRECTIONS FOR HIGHER EDUCATION • DOI: 10.1002/he

1

This chapter presents an overview of current issues related to distance learning in higher education. It identifies central questions, issues, challenges, and opportunities that must be addressed by decision makers, as well as key attributes of effective leaders.

Issues in Distance Education: A Primer for Higher Education Decision Makers

Michael Beaudoin

The theme of this publication prompted me to peruse my professional library for books with similar titles alluding to the future of higher education, to discern what attention authors gave to distance education in this context. Arthur Levine's book, *Shaping Higher Education's Future* (1989), made no mention whatsoever of distance education, technology, or any related subjects. Fifteen years later, Newman, Couturier, and Scurry in *The Future of Higher Education* (2004) did devote three pages to online education, primarily presenting statistics reflecting the growth of online enrollments, and acknowledged that "learning via the Internet can be both effective and satisfying for students, when done well" (p. 20). In a subsequent three-page section, the authors prognosticated about the future of instructional technology, stating that faculty remain wary of this development, and that use of this resource within the classroom is likely to be where and how it has its most significant impact. This chapter uses the term *online education* to refer to teaching and learning via technology-enhanced devices.

Beginning in the first decade of the new millennium, a spate of new books did finally begin to examine the present and future role of technology-assisted teaching and learning at the postsecondary level, both within and beyond the United States (Beaudoin, 2006; Duderstadt, Atkins, & Van Houweling, 2002; Nata, 2005; Rovai, Ponton, & Baker, 2008), and this interest has not waned since those volumes initially addressed this burgeoning worldwide phenomenon. Delving further into the growing body of literature in this field, at least three discernible themes seem to be emerging, especially in the more opinion-based commentary about the future of online education: one that treats this development as if it is a trend likely to eventually affect the future of higher education, but one unlikely to have a positive impact. Another perspective acknowledges, albeit somewhat begrudgingly, that online education has already insinuated itself into the conventional educational environment, and although such courses are becoming more acceptable as a valid form of postsecondary education, they have yet to prove their efficacy. And the third theme enthusiastically chronicles the impressive gains and benefits of expanded offerings delivered anytime and anyplace utilizing instructional technology.

At one end of this continuum, we detect what some might argue is an overly sanguine view of what distance education has already achieved and how much it has influenced pedagogy and the academy. At the other extreme is the pessimistic perspective that this phenomenon is a scourge threatening the quality and integrity of academe. One would like to believe that any academic leader, teacher or scholar in this digital age, in which the number of students taking at least one online course continues to grow annually at a rate far in excess of overall enrollments (Allen & Seaman, 2014), would see this trend as one that clearly enriches the college experience and expands educational opportunities, rather than one that many still perceive to be a threat to rigorous academics. If institutional decision makers predict a phase of unprecedented innovation that is enhancing learning for a new generation of students, then surely they should recognize and acknowledge the obvious role of online education in achieving this goal.

Threats and Opportunities

Yet, despite the naysayers, resisters, and others who continue to lurk on the periphery of distance education, we can detect much evidence of solid success in this arena, as institutions worldwide engage in this exciting practice to bring educational opportunities via virtual and other means to learners, both close and distant. The presumed innovative phase over the next 20 years when traditional ideas and arrangements in higher education will be challenged and transformed to effectively engage learners anytime and anyplace has already occurred and has had a decisive impact on many institutions and their stakeholders.

Certainly, there are questionable programs and products, often fueled by the appetite for expanded market share and profit regardless of quality. In this regard, the burgeoning for-profit sector of online higher education invites criticisms of allegedly sacrificing quality for quantity. Whether this is deserved or not, it is important to recognize that for-profit entities do not have the monopoly on less-than-ideal online course content and delivery. No educational provider—large or small, nonprofit or for-profit, local or international, private or public—is immune from unethical behavior and disservice to those it serves. As higher education providers develop and deliver online education to greater numbers of learners not previously served, there is risk of increased vulnerability of both providers and users due to missteps each may take into unfamiliar territory.

NEW DIRECTIONS FOR HIGHER EDUCATION • DOI: 10.1002/he

But perhaps more alarming than the occasional failed effort at launching distance education products is the pervasive resistance, and in many cases the outright hostility toward any movement in the direction of alternative ways of teaching and learning. Many in key leadership roles continue to demonstrate a startling lack of insight into the power and promise of, in particular, online education now occurring at all educational levels. While some are finally touting their institutions' progress in designing and delivering more online courses, strong skepticism stubbornly prevails, as evidenced, for example, by the comments in *Time* magazine (Reif, 2013) of the president of a major institution who, while extolling the virtues of online courses, clearly reveals his lingering doubt in suggesting that digital learning is not as good as true education transmitted face-to-face, in achieving a close personal connection with an inspiring mentor; in developing judgment, confidence, teamwork, and writing and analytical skills; and in exploring ideas, ethics, and values. Another university president, in an interview with *Money* magazine (Regnier, 2013), stated that students sitting at home watching professors talk on their laptops is not an education, and that those who just learn from a computer, as compared to students who actually interact with professors, would be a "social disaster" (p. 83). The implication here is that online study cannot possibly be as good as what occurs in a classroom, the latter venue typically cited as the exemplar to emulate for quality instruction. This is despite the fact that many recent studies and reports have consistently found that a growing majority of chief academic officers rate the learning outcomes for online education "as good as or better than" those for face-to-face instruction (Allen & Seaman, 2014).

Arguably, Internet-supported teaching and learning are the most important innovation in education since the printing press. In this context, it is encouraging to see more endorsements of online education as a means of making college cheaper, more accessible, and better, coming from increasing numbers of leaders of major U.S. institutions of higher education, and yet, too often, their remarks still reveal the hesitation they have in going so far as to state that digital learning is as good as education provided face-to-face, or that it can achieve a close personal connection with a teacher; can develop sound judgment, confidence, teamwork, and writing and analytical skills; and can effectively explore ideas, ethics, and values. As long as influential educators imply that such attributes and skills are best acquired by students gathered together in a classroom, dutifully listening to an instructor lecturing at the front of the room, online education's legitimate role in advancing the personal goals and professional aspirations of diverse learners will be compromised.

And when those who guide the future of the higher education sector maintain a watchful waiting stance, speculating about what opportunities digital learning technologies might eventually provide, and imagining what colleges might look like in the future, they reflect an embarrassing ignorance of what has already arrived. It is as if they are standing on the shore, vigilantly watching for a tsunami that is inexorably moving toward them, somehow missing the reality that the future they envision is already upon them. Many of the changes they contemplate, such as a blending of online and face-to-face instruction, are occurring at a dramatic pace worldwide. Indeed, many such encroachments on conventional education, enabled by instructional technology, may be much more in place within their own institutions than they realize. This lack of awareness may reflect a bias that some educators continue to view higher education as an experience limited to students sitting in classrooms. Yet, like it or not, online numbers now represent the majority of new postsecondary course enrollments each year in the United States, and at present constitute slightly more than one third of all enrollments (Allen & Seaman, 2014).

In short, what is being intimated here is that perhaps the greatest threat to the future role of distance education within the higher education sphere is not so much self-immolation inflicted on themselves by well-intentioned innovators who simply lack the knowledge and skill to launch and sustain sound distance education projects, or acts of sabotage executed by those who actively oppose such efforts. Rather, the threat more insidiously lurks within the political, economic, and academic power centers that represent and protect their self-interests by preserving the status quo (i.e., the conventional way of doing business in academe, buttressed by decades of espousing new ideas and practices that are not reflected in the day-to-day manner in which they operate). It is a climate often characterized by fear that the hegemony long enjoyed by higher education might be supplanted by the emergence of a digital world that does not need to rely on tradition any longer.

Despite the occupational hazards noted, the opportunities may well be worth the risk, if explored and executed with informed judgment, ethical behavior, and a commitment to quality. There are realms where the higher education community might pursue new options for innovation and growth. In the current era, many institutions are aggressively expanding their online offerings, even across international boundaries, thus creating new encounters between stakeholders, both providers and consumers, attempting to achieve their respective organizational and personal goals. Following is a short list of prospective opportunities that distance education decision makers might consider as they explore new avenues for the future. Any such list could, of course, be much longer, but those noted here are proffered because they have the power to create a ripple effect in that they have the potential to achieve significant impact within the distance education field.

International Programs.   There is a long tradition of cross-cultural efforts to diffuse technology-supported education across boundaries to unfamiliar places distant from the point of delivery. This is arguably one of the most critical areas for distance educators to explore as we rapidly evolve into a global society. Those who have considered and/or are engaged in this activity must know what Bentley (1993) refers to as "patterns of cross-cultural conversion, conflict and compromise" (p. vii). He notes that this is a complicated process, but one that has the potential to bring about transformation. Accordingly, those involved must be well informed about the nuances that affect, positively and negatively, the diffusion of online education involving individuals and entities representing differing cultural traditions. (Note: Chapters 8 and 9 in this issue examine this phenomenon in some depth.)

Partnerships.   There is a strong case for choosing collaboration over competition as an essential arrangement for achieving the greatest potential of distance education. Such strategic alliances reflect a variety of arrangements; consortia appear to be a preferred form of interinstitutional partnerships to implement and sustain distance education, particularly for courses and services offered across national and cultural boundaries. Consortia can encompass a variety of private and public institutions offering online courses and/or degrees distributed over vast areas and serving diverse learners. Whatever the venue, partners should possess compatible practices, values, ethics, and goals. International alliances can overcome barriers of language, culture, accreditation, articulation, and student support (Beaudoin, 2013). In all contexts, a clear and comprehensive agreement is essential for effective development and operation of partnerships. Planning these collaborations typically takes more time than anticipated, but with adequate resources, support, and time, new opportunities not feasible by single providers become viable, and can attract increasing numbers of students and faculty, as well as financial support from varied sources, not likely available to a sole entity.

Advancing Distance Education.   Many distance education initiatives have ultimately enjoyed success, even when introduced into organizational settings that were not especially receptive. Such efforts have resulted in significant enrollments, increasing expertise in designing and delivering online offerings, a growing cadre of skilled instructors, and a viable infrastructure to ensure quality and sustain the investment. Yet, it is not uncommon for such successful enterprises recognized as epicenters of innovative programming to remain anomalies within their home institutions. In an ideal environment, innovative educators seek means to utilize instructional technology as a tool for building collective knowledge through pedagogical renewal, rather than perpetuate debilitating aspects of the prevailing educational system. But the demands of one's immediate roles and responsibilities at the program level typically preclude more ambitious agendas.

Advocating and advancing the distance education agenda at the broader institutional level, though not always pursued, presents an opportunity for replication of these solid accomplishments at a macro level. This should not be seen as an effort to supplant conventional practices, but rather, through influencing subtle shifts in the campus culture, it is a means of sharing the benefits realized at the program level with a wider

NEW DIRECTIONS FOR HIGHER EDUCATION • DOI: 10.1002/he

constituency, hopefully enhancing an institution's overall value, generating additional revenues, and expanding its markets to ensure long-term viability.

Preparing the Next Generation of Distance Educators.   A related opportunity, indeed perhaps an obligation for today's more experienced distance education practitioners, is the important work of preparing the next generation to move into the field. Many who have been successful in the development and institutionalization of distance education up to this point gravitated to it, whether by design or default, via other roles in higher education, such as continuing education. This transition has not been especially easy for many, often involving trial and error, lonely labors with few allies, and perhaps a long learning curve to arrive at a rewarding place and to feel any real sense of accomplishment. At this juncture, as the field has gained legitimacy and widespread adoption, it is crucial that the next generation of teachers, administrators, instructional designers, scholars, and others aspiring to have an impact in key roles begin their work early in their academic careers, rather than as a later capstone activity. Through conferences and seminars, degree programs with curricula fashioned to provide expertise in this field of practice, mature mentors who guide energetic new aspirants, as well as exposure to theory and best practices through sound research and writing, there is a tremendous opportunity to further advance distance education to the next stage of its remarkable progress thus far.

It should be noted, too, that an important sector of the higher education community needing nurturing is faculty who persist in their resistance to, and skepticism of, online teaching and learning. Certainly, an impressive cadre of distance educators from traditional faculty ranks has evolved at many institutions, and yet, many remain unaware of the exciting advantages available to them and to their students by adopting and adapting web-based resources into classroom-based courses, and converting their courses into online formats. In the not-too-distant past, most college professors avoided chronicling on their curriculum vitae any online experience they might have acquired; now, most of them tout this skill to make themselves more marketable and to increase their job security. It is important that instructors recognize the benefits of moving into this brave new world before they miss entirely this opportunity for further professional development that might also enhance their face-to-face pedagogy.

Distance Education as Disruptive Innovation

However noble our agenda to advance alternative means and modes of teaching and learning might be, decision makers and others active in the field must be cognizant that what we do, to use Clayton Christensen's (1997) terminology, is *disruptive innovation*, and thus is often understandably perceived as an inherent threat to the status quo in academe, and so is likely to engender powerful forces resisting any change. To assume that the growing acceptance of online education assures success with whatever endeavor we launch is not simply naive; it also sets up those aspiring to introduce change for a fall that may preclude them from achieving any positive outcomes now or in the future.

Traditional academic institutions are an indispensable cornerstone of society and culture because the college experience is transformative for so many people. Yet ironically, the higher education sector is firmly entrenched in a legacy that has persevered for a millennium, and is typically resistant to any significant change. There is obvious irony in the fact that although the college experience can be transformative for so many people, the learning organization is inherently resistant to transforming itself. Although difficult to abandon a model that has changed little since its inception, competition from the rapidly growing for-profit higher education sector, as well as diminishing resources and higher costs, has created a sense of urgency. Indeed, for some institutions, their very survival may require them to reconstitute themselves in order to become more responsive and relevant to new demands from a clientele reflecting an evolving demographic profile. The conundrum for these institutions is that alterations needed to move them into the arena of online learning technologies that can potentially benefit them can also create temporary disruption for them in the early stages of a change process. It may be only eventually and perhaps gradually that this investment creates new opportunities that lead them and their stakeholders to greater prosperity and benefits. Ultimately, a positive outcome is likely to depend on whether they attempt to revert back to a model that has changed little since its founding, or they adopt, if not fully embrace, learning innovations made possible by new technology.

Throughout his influential work on innovation and change, Christensen (1997) refers to the *innovator's dilemma*, noting the irony of how many successful organizations are often the most resistant to change because their leaders believe they represent the avant-garde, having already introduced innovations that have led to profit and prestige. This self-perception, even if reasonably accurate, tends to reduce incentive for contemplating further changes. Christensen and Eyring (2011) have applied the notion of disruptive technology specifically to higher education, best illustrated in its initially cautious response, as we have noted, to the Internet and its learning potential, followed by its adoption once it becomes more apparent that making teaching and learning possible at anytime and anyplace is increasingly accepted and legitimized. Regardless of how much online education has insinuated itself into higher education's domain, it has unavoidably fostered some disruptive change. Decision makers who are resilient and less risk averse have typically fared better than their more timid counterparts in this process.

Christensen makes the distinction between disruptive innovation and sustaining innovation. While introducing any authentic innovation is likely disruptive, it is the leadership's ultimate challenge to institutionalize it to become a sustaining innovation. Even strong and stable organizations are vulnerable to failure when confronted with disruptive changes, whether driven by technology or by other innovative forces. A successful institution may fail because it attempts to respond to new technology to satisfy a new market (e.g., online offerings to appeal to older, distant students) but, in doing so, it might lose its reputational position with established clientele (e.g., existing campus-based students and their tuition-paying parents). Seemingly logical decisions critical to success can be the same ones that cause loss of position against competition. For this reason alone, many education providers eschew opportunities to implement even relatively modest distance education initiatives while their competition boldly advances into this exciting arena. This is the innovator's dilemma!

Distance Education as Transformation

Transforming a disruptive innovation into a sustaining one entails significant adaptation, and leadership is the crucial ingredient. Because disruptive technologies typically require time between investing in them and profiting from them, aside from the distinct possibility that success may never be realized, decision makers can quickly conjure up arguments for maintaining the status quo. The conflicting demands of disruptive and sustaining technologies require leaders with the capacity to resolve those tensions, and to create a context and culture in which, and by which, the differing challenges faced by innovators become less of a dilemma, and more of a transformative environment for productive and meaningful change.

Distance education leadership can be defined as creating the conditions for innovative change. The primary task is not, as many aspiring decision makers may assume, one of managing technology, but rather managing change. In this context, leadership is an inherently transformative process and, as such, demands that every player, whether involved in a developing program or in a more established entity, understands and executes the principles and practices of transformation. These are distinct from (and more complex than) the transitional process of merely managing and contributing to the functions that sustain an operation and optimize its efficiency. The truly transformative distance educator engages other key stakeholders in all phases of the change process, fostering a culture of innovative and productive growth with the least amount of disruption, while having the maximum influence and impact at both the micro level (e.g., online program) and the macro level (e.g., the entire institution).

If we accept the premise that distance education, in its many evolving manifestations, is having an increasingly transformative impact on how higher education has evolved from its historical medieval model to what Peters (1994) refers to as an industrial model (i.e., a division of labor in course development, production, and delivery), then we can make the case that distance education's decision makers and the teams they lead have been responsible for fairly widespread disruptive innovation in this historically placid environment, particularly over the past 20 or so years. This has surely demanded distance education practitioners with appropriate attributes to effectively address the many challenges confronting them as they have moved their institutions into the digital age.

Distance Education Challenges and Attributes

So what, then, are some of the most daunting challenges facing higher education decision makers determined to move their followers and their institutions further into the digital age, and what are the attributes that might best equip them for success in achieving their goals? Providers of online education—whether administrators, program planners, instructional designers, teachers, student support personnel, or others in key roles—all are faced with formidable challenges to ensure that education and training delivered at a distance remain accessible and relevant. The issues that higher education leaders are likely to be confronted with, especially in the constantly evolving sphere of online education, are varied and complex, and often subtle but significant. Some challenges that are ignored or responded to ineffectively may have minimum consequences for institutions, their leaders, and their stakeholders, but others, if not adequately addressed, can be disastrous and can compromise both immediate and longer-range success. Among those that can be most vexing are:

- Contending with a changing learner landscape, reflecting new needs and demands.
- Monitoring and reducing the so-called digital divide that separates resources from prospective users.
- Enhancing access for users and opportunity for providers without compromising quality.
- Resolving the frequent tension between technology and pedagogy.
- Determining effective applications of social networks for learning.
- Overcoming persistent faculty resistance to adoption of online instruction.
- Achieving authentic assessments of learning outcomes in online settings.
- Balancing issues of academic freedom and intellectual property in online course development.
- Countering the prevailing myths in the distance education field that perpetuate hostility.
- Resisting the influence of others with limited expertise in online education.
- Navigating the hazards of regulatory initiatives and other impediments to growth.
- Getting complex new programs functioning quickly within environments with no precedents.

- Interacting with diverse partners, some with little or no experience in online education.
- Directing teams in accomplishing multiple tasks, often with pressing deadlines.
- Identifying and implementing suitable virtual teaching/learning tools for optimum effectiveness.

What characteristics and qualities are especially critical to those responsible for advancing and sustaining distance education, while at the same time also maneuvering the gauntlet of challenges just noted? Are there certain attributes that distance education practitioners should possess to be effective in this complex milieu? There is not, of course, any definitive list of knowledge and skills, or formulaic recommendations of how best to ensure success in addressing the challenges noted, or others we might add to this already formidable list, but those suggested next are worthy of consideration. These items are intended to convey a sense of qualities a leader is likely to need to succeed and, in some instances, perhaps even to survive:

- Commit to a transformative leadership style.
- Be able to create conditions for innovation and change.
- Recognize that the priority is managing change, rather than technology.
- Possess sound knowledge of distance education theory and practice.
- Have patience, resilience, dedication, and tolerance for ambiguity and risk.
- Be able to distinguish between and utilize both strategic and tactical planning.
- Apply diagnostic skills to assess situations before acting.
- Utilize data for decision making.
- Focus on both the micro and macro perspectives.
- Operationalize one's vision, not just espouse it.
- Be an articulate and informed advocate of distance education.
- Value and engage in networking, sharing ideas, strategies, and resources.
- Be enterprising, but resist early adoption of what is currently in vogue.
- Maintain a commitment to quality.
- Always decide and act as a learner-centered educator.

Conclusion

While this work does not pretend to address every challenge that distance educators face in this digital age, or reveal precisely what needs to be done (and how) to meet every challenge, it is hoped that it does offer a valuable perspective on an aspect of the field that demands expertise and insight to succeed, especially among those in leadership roles. The contents offer a range of issues and strategies needed to effectively guide institutional involvement in distance education, and should provide clear evidence that the future of higher education is, and will continue to be, positively impacted by the increasing role of instructional technology resources offered worldwide to diverse learners, ideally in concert with more traditional means of transmitting knowledge and skills. It is hoped that this work further contributes to the advancement of worthwhile research and effective practice, and also provokes further thought and action in this arena. But this burgeoning phenomenon of distance education cannot be adequately sustained and its effectiveness ensured unless we understand the issues, engage in competent practice, and benefit from strong leadership in the field. The work we are engaged in is too important not to rise to this challenge.

References

Allen, E., & Seaman, J. (2014). *Grade change: Tracking online education in the United States.* Babson Park, MA: Babson Survey Research Group and Quahog Research Group. http://sloanconsortium.org/publications/survey/grade-change-2013

Beaudoin, M. (2013). Leadership challenges in trans-cultural online education. In I. Jung & C. Gunawardena (Eds.), *Culture and online learning: Global perspectives and research* (pp. 115–125). Sterling, VA: Stylus Publishing.

Beaudoin, M. (Ed.). (2006). *Perspectives on the future of higher education in the digital age.* Hauppauge, NY: Nova Science Publishers.

Bentley, J. (1993). *Old world encounters.* Oxford, UK: Oxford University Press.

Christensen, C. (1997). *The innovator's dilemma: When new technologies cause great firms to fail.* Cambridge, MA: Harvard Business School Press.

Christensen, C., & Eyring, H. (2011). *The innovative university: Changing the DNA of higher education from the inside out.* San Francisco, CA: Jossey-Bass.

Duderstadt, J., Atkins, D., & Van Houweling, D. (2002). *Higher education in the digital age.* Westport, CT: Praeger Publishers.

Levine, A., et al. (1989). *Shaping higher education's future.* San Francisco, CA: Jossey-Bass.

Nata, R. (Ed.). (2005). *Issues in higher education.* New York: Nova Science Publishers.

Newman, F., Couturier, L., & Scurry, J. (2004). *The future of higher education.* San Francisco, CA: Jossey-Bass.

Peters, O. (1994). *Otto Peters on distance education: The industrialization of teaching and learning.* K. Desmond (Ed.): Abingdon, UK: Psychology Press.

Regnier, P. (2013, August). Does college still pay off? *Money,* 80–83.

Reif, R. (2013, October 7). Online learning will make college cheaper. It will also make it better. *Time,* 54–55.

Rovai, A., Ponton, M., & Baker, J. (2008). *Distance learning in higher education.* New York: Columbia Teachers College Press.

MICHAEL BEAUDOIN *is professor emeritus of education at the University of New England. He has developed and directed several distance/online education degree programs and courses, and is the author of more than 100 publications on distance education and related topics.*

2

This chapter presents an overview of theories of distance education and discusses their implications for future policy making and practice in institutions of higher education.

Theories of Distance Education: Why They Matter

Farhad Saba

The advent of correspondence education in the 1860s ushered in the era of distance education; however, systematic study of distance education as a distinct academic discipline is of more recent vintage. Even though theorists from Australia, Great Britain, Canada, Germany, Sweden, and the United States have been contributing to its conceptual development over the past 50 years, it was not until 1980 that its first formal academic journal surfaced. That was the year that Desmond Keegan, a pioneering scholar and practitioner in the field, launched the publication of the journal *Distance Education* in Australia. Michael G. Moore, one of the leading theorists in the field, established the *American Journal of Distance Education* a few years later in 1987.

Keegan (1996) characterized distance education as a distinct and separate area of practice and study from mainstream traditional education, stating:

> Distance education is a coherent and distinct field of educational endeavor: it embraces programmes at a distance at primary and secondary, technical and further, college and university levels in both public and private sectors. It has existed for a hundred years and is to be found today in most countries (p. 12).

Although distance education may resemble mainstream traditional education, its philosophical and theoretical foundations as well as its methods of practice are distinct. Because of this similarity, the phrase *distance education* is often misconstrued to mean nothing more than a form of traditional education enhanced by information and communication technologies. From its outset, distance education was differentiated from traditional education by serving nontraditional learners. Charles Wedemeyer, professor emeritus, University of Wisconsin–Madison, a leading theorist and

NEW DIRECTIONS FOR HIGHER EDUCATION, no. 173, Spring 2016 © 2016 Wiley Periodicals, Inc.
Published online in Wiley Online Library (wileyonlinelibrary.com) • DOI: 10.1002/he.20176

visionary in the field, asserted that traditional institutions of education actually impede learning. He included K–12 schools, colleges, and universities. Wedemeyer posited that traditional education is relatively new in human history and carries with it anachronisms imposed from earlier eras. One such holdover still in effect, starting the academic year in the fall (after the harvest), stems from the agricultural era. Another, offering instruction in standardized time intervals of 45 minutes, is an artifact of the industrial era. Nontraditional learning methods afforded by distance education eliminate such restrictions. They increase responsiveness to the academic needs of the learner while reducing the cost of going to college and the time to obtain a degree. They serve the needs of individual learners by offering them personal autonomy that leads to creative thinking and innovation. The true differences, Wedemeyer (1981) wrote,

> are to be found in the capacity of non-traditional learning to tolerate and exploit physical distance between teacher and learner; in the invention and discovery of learning models that transcend the traditional; in a new understanding of the learning environment, so that a learner does not have to be in a specific place at a specific time to enjoy opportunity and access for learning; in a new perception of time with respect to the stages of learning; in the consistent effort to place the learner in the center of the teaching-learning process, with more active and responsible roles; in roles for teachers that link teaching with more truly professional activities, in concepts of instructional design and institutional development that are based more on fulfilling learning requirements and activities than on teaching requirements and activities (p. xxii).

Today, the profiles of most students in institutions of higher education are closer to that of the nontraditional learner. They work at least part-time, if not full-time; they have family responsibilities; and they are active in various institutions of civil society in addition to being students. Increasingly, they see themselves as members of a global community of learners who help each other in solving problems—small and large—at the speed of the Internet.

A keynote of distance education is that its theorists see the world of learning and teaching from the point of view of the learner. They may express the centrality of the learner in the process of education (learning and teaching) in different ways; however, they agree that learning is a personal and individual act, with the instructor playing a key role in facilitating learning. At the macro level, the instructor balances the learner's desire for autonomy by providing the organization and structure of an academic discipline.

Borje Holmberg (1993) used the term *empathy* to highlight the role of the instructor. He stated:

> Basically, empathy in our context seems to denote the capacity and readiness to experience and, as it were, personally feel students' uncertainty, anxiety,

hesitation, on the one hand, their confidence, intellectual pleasure and *"eureka"* sensations on the other hand, and share these experiences with them (pp. 336–337).

To Holmberg, the primary role of the instructor is to empathize with the learner. The secondary role of the instructor is to impart information to students when necessary.

In *Theory and Practice of Distance Education,* Holmberg (1995) proposed the concept of guided didactic conversation as a "pervasive characteristic of distance education" (p. 47). He emphasized the importance of a "feeling of personal relation between the teacher and learner" (p. 47) and postulated that if personal communication between the learner and instructor takes place in the framework of a "friendly conversation" (p. 47) students understand and remember instructional information easily. Such conversations facilitate the organization of study material as well as the achievement of the implicit and explicit instructional goals. Also, by offering professionally designed and developed self-instructional materials, the instructor can bolster this "feeling of personal relation" through two-way media of communication. Thus, Holmberg established the principle that personal communication between the learner and the instructor is an essential cornerstone of the theory of distance education.

With the ideas and theories of Wedemeyer and Holmberg as a bridge, Moore further developed the theoretical foundations of distance education when he conceptualized the *theory of transactional distance* (Moore, 2013). In this theory, distance between the learner and the instructor is not a set geographic space measured by miles or kilometers. It is a psychological distance that varies by the modulation of three constructs: *autonomy, structure,* and *dialogue.* These constructs are measured by the quality and quantity of communication between the instructor and the learner. According to Moore (1983):

- *Dialogue* describes the extent to which, in any educational program, learner and educator are able to respond to each other. This is determined by the content or subject matter that is studied, by the educational philosophy of the educator, by the personalities of educator and learner, and by environmental factors, the most important of which is the medium of communication (p. 157).
- *Structure* is a measure of an educational program's responsiveness to a learner's individual needs. It expresses the extent to which educational objectives, teaching strategies, and evaluation methods are prepared for, or can be adapted to the objectives, strategies, and evaluation methods of the learner. In a highly structured educational program, the objectives and the methods to be used are determined for the learner and are inflexible (p. 157).
- *Autonomy* refers to the extent to which learners decide on certain factors such as "what to learn, how to learn, and how much to learn" (p. 68).

Moore posited that adult learners tend to set their own learning goals and pursue such goals on their own. He set forward two kinds of autonomy—emotional and instrumental—and defined them as follows:

> Instrumental independence involves the ability to undertake an activity, including learning, without seeking help; emotional independence is the capacity to pursue the activity without seeking reassurance, affection or approval in order to complete it. The drive to achievement is derived from a need for self-approval (Moore, 1983, p. 162).

As Moore postulated, and Saba and Shearer (1994) demonstrated in an experimental study, there is an inverse relationship between dialogue and structure. When dialogue increases, structure and the level of transactional distance decrease. When structure increases, dialogue decreases, but transactional distance increases as well. Autonomy is measured by variables related to learner control, such as when a learner asks a direct question. Structure is quantified by variables related to instructor control, such as when an instructor provides specific directions to learners. In offering individual adaptive learning experiences, the variability of transactional distance is based on structure, dialogue, and autonomy and the subordinate variables to each of these three key constructs. As such, distance in education varies for individual learners during the course of instruction depending on their personal readiness for autonomy and need for structure. The level of such distance is value neutral, and its only utility is enhancing learning. Structure and transactional distance may be high at the beginning of a course when the instructor is setting the learning agenda and describing the nature of the discipline to learners. As individual learners become more knowledgeable and skilled, structure for each tends to decrease, thus decreasing transactional distance. While a general pattern for such modulation is in evidence in experimental studies, each learner shows a different pattern for readiness for more autonomy and less structure as the learner moves from being a novice to becoming an expert. Consideration of these factors will have significant ramifications for future teaching practices and institutional organization. These will be discussed in the following sections.

Ramifications for the Organization of Colleges and Universities

Offering adaptive learning that is designed and developed to respond to the needs of the individual learner for structure, dialogue, and autonomy can be implemented in those educational organizations that have flexible management systems. The current rigid management practices in higher education evolved to their present form during the industrial era when flexibility was equated with lack of standards. These practices, however, proved quite efficient during the second half of the 20th century when enrollments sharply increased. Administrators were able to manage the mass convergence of presence. These key concepts are instrumental in facilitating learning in a community of instructors and learners.

1. *Social presence* is "the ability to project one's self and establish personal and purposeful relationships. The three main aspects of social presence, as defined here, are effective communication, open communication and group cohesion" (Garrison, 2007, p. 63).
2. *Cognitive presence* is "the exploration, construction, resolution and confirmation of understanding through collaboration and reflection in a community of inquiry" (Garrison, 2007, p. 65).
3. *Teaching presence* is "the design, facilitation and direction of cognitive and social processes for the purpose of realizing personally meaningful and educationally worthwhile learning outcomes" (Anderson, Rourke, Garrison, & Archer, 2001, p. 5).

COI's theoretical lineage traces back to Wedemeyer and Harasim. While Wedemeyer saw the individual learner as an active, self-directed, and full participant in the process of teaching and learning, Harasim and Gunawardena emphasized the social nature of learning. Later, COI researchers Swan, Garrison, and Richardson (2009) focused on the dynamic balance among social, cognitive, and teaching presences during a course of study. They found that guidance by an instructor in a community was vital to the process of teaching and learning. However, the role of participants in a class or a course of study is not static. Learners at times become teachers, and teachers learn from their learners. In the traditional models of education, the focus is on how the subject matter is structured and presented by the instructor. In nontraditional education, the learner can be an equal participant in the process of learning and teaching, although the instructor must ensure that the community observes the structure and integrity of the academic discipline. The learner's voice is increasingly amplified in the contemporary social media environment. Although educational applications of personal media, ranging from broadcasting video on the Internet to socializing on Twitter or Facebook, are in their infancy, they have already provided means of communication to the learner that were available to very few professional broadcasters and journalists and even fewer educators in decades past.

Conclusion

Because of the ubiquity of information and communication technology, higher education will not be confined to a set time and place. However, information and communication technology in itself does not determine how it is to be used. We may choose to use it to support and amplify the current management system of higher education, offer less choice, increase the cost to the taxpayer and students, and extend the time that it takes for students to graduate. Another way of using information and communication technology is to develop curricula and programs that are based on the theoretical foundations of distance education. Differential learning programs and flexible schedules increase choices for learners, provide each individual learner the degree of autonomy and structure the learner needs to excel, and place each learner in a supportive community of instructors and peers that would lead to generating and validating new knowledge.

References

Anderson, T., Rourke, L., Garrison, D. R., & Archer, W. (2001). Assessing teaching presence in a computer conferencing context. *Journal of Asynchronous Learning Networks*, 5(2). Retrieved from http://www.sloan-c.org/publications/jaln/v5n2/index.asp

Bell, D. (1973). *The coming of the post-industrial society: A venture in future forecasting.* New York: Basic Books.

Garrison, D. R. (2007). Online community of inquiry review: Social, cognitive, and teaching presence issues. *Journal of Asynchronous Learning Networks*, 11(1). Retrieved from http://sloanconsortium.org/jaln/v11n1/online-community-inquiry-review-social-cognitive-and-teaching-presence-issues

Garrison, D. R., Anderson, T., & Archer, W. (2000). Critical inquiry in a text-based environment: Computer conferencing in higher education. *Internet and Higher Education*, 2(2–3), 87–105.

Gunawardena, C. N. (1995). Social presence theory and implications for interaction and collaborative learning in computer conferences. *International Journal of Educational Telecommunications*, 1(2). Retrieved from http://www.editlib.org/p/15156

Harasim, L. (1990). *Online education: Perspectives on a new environment.* New York: Praeger.

Holmberg, B. (1993). Key issues in distance education: An academic perspective. In K. Harry, M. John, & D. Keegan (Eds.), *Distance education: New perspectives* (pp. 330–341). London, UK: Routledge.

Holmberg, B. (1995). *Theory and practice of distance education.* New York: Routledge.

Keegan, D. (1996). *Foundations of distance education* (3rd ed.). New York: Routledge.

Moore, M. G. (1983). The individual adult learner. In M. Tight (Ed.), *Adult learning and education* (pp. 153–168). London, UK: Croom Helm.

Moore, M. G. (1989). Three types of interaction. *American Journal of Distance Education*, 3(2), 1–6.

Moore, M. G. (2013). The theory of transactional distance. In M. G. Moore (Ed.), *Handbook of distance education* (3rd ed., pp. 66–85). New York: Routledge.

Mumford, L. (1934). *Techniques and civilization.* New York: Harcourt Brace.

Saba, F., & Shearer, R. L. (1994). Verifying key theoretical concepts in a dynamic model of distance education. *American Journal of Distance Education*, 8(1), 36–59.

Saettler, P. (1990). *The evolution of American educational technology.* Englewood, CO: Libraries Unlimited.

Swan, K., Garrison, D. R., & Richardson, J. C. (2009). A constructivist approach to online learning: The community of inquiry framework. In C. R. Payne (Ed.), *Information technology and constructivism in higher education: Progressive learning frameworks* (pp. 43–57). Hershey, PA: IGI Global.

Toffler, A. (1980). *The third wave.* New York: Bantam Books.

Wedemeyer, C. A. (1981). *Learning at the back door: Reflections on non-traditional learning in the lifespan.* Madison, WI: University of Wisconsin Press.

FARHAD SABA *is professor emeritus of educational technology at San Diego State University.*

3

This chapter describes organizational structures and processes at the institutional and project levels for the development and support of distance learning initiatives. It addresses environmental and stakeholder issues and explores principles and strategies of effective leadership for change creation and management.

Effective Organizational Structures and Processes: Addressing Issues of Change

Maureen Snow Andrade

Distance learning has individual, institutional, national, and global benefits. It improves social equity by extending access to underrepresented populations (White, 2005), and reaching those who have been historically marginalized "to change lives and improve communities and economies" (Andrade, 2013, p. 67). Distance learning is becoming mainstream in higher education (Beaudoin, 2013) due to increasing demand and improved technologies.

Distance learning infrastructures may have developed rapidly and haphazardly or gradually and strategically, depending on response to opportunities to innovate, meet demand, or compete. Both macro, or institutional, organizational structures and micro, or project-level, structures must be considered relative to these initiatives. This chapter examines structure, external and internal environments, and leadership principles and strategies for change.

Macro- or Institutional-Level Structures

Administrators must consider the advantages and disadvantages of various organizational frameworks and determine those best suited to their vision. Decisions must also consider stakeholders and encourage collaboration. The following discussion reviews possible organizational structures for the development and delivery of distance education programs.

Centralized and Decentralized. Centralized structures typically involve a distance education unit with instructional designers, media and graphic experts, and technology specialists. Faculty members provide

NEW DIRECTIONS FOR HIGHER EDUCATION, no. 173, Spring 2016 © 2016 Wiley Periodicals, Inc.
Published online in Wiley Online Library (wileyonlinelibrary.com) • DOI: 10.1002/he.20177

31

content expertise, and instructional designers contribute delivery and design options. Centralized units offer assistance from the conceptual stage through enrollment, ongoing technology and course support, and evaluation. Those responsible for these units must view "themselves, and be seen, as educational leaders who, through less directing and more motivating, facilitate the articulation, development, implementation, and stewardship of a vision of learning that is shared and supported by a wider academic community" (Beaudoin, 2013, p. 476).

Advantages of the centralized model are consistency, quality, and control to ensure that online learners receive similar content, rigor, and support as face-to-face students (Eskey, 2010). The model is cost-effective as it entails supporting a single organizational unit rather than multiple operations (Eskey, 2010). It provides consistent instructor training, instruction, and evaluation; is responsive to student and faculty needs; and ensures appropriate workforce credentials. Administrators favor this model.

Faculty may prefer a decentralized model that allows greater autonomy over content and design as well as operational logistics such as marketing, recruitment, scheduling, and assessment. Independent distance education units may increase faculty motivation to participate but could result in inconsistent quality and a lack of overall institutional strategy. Although university administrators view the quality of distance learning courses as equivalent to face-to-face instruction, they estimate that only about 30% of their faculty agrees (Allen & Seaman, 2013). Thus, skepticism or even resistance toward distance learning is an issue, and initiatives may not flourish in a decentralized model.

A decentralized model is characterized by operations within departments or colleges, which market, recruit, and manage courses. Development may occur at the faculty or department level and involve collaboration with technology, the learning management system, or curriculum specialists. A distinct disadvantage of the decentralized model is that instructors focus on their own courses rather than contributing to a well-conceived institution-wide effort. The decentralized "approach will not result in a system-wide adoption of distance education in any comprehensive and cost-effective manner" (Beaudoin, 2013, p. 475).

Many institutions have a mixed system with some aspects of development such as course design, media, training, and delivery under a distance education unit, and curriculum, hiring, and scheduling under academic departments. In some cases, faculty develop courses with design and technology specialists, and the distance education unit hires off-site faculty, with department approval, to teach the courses. Other institutions outsource operations completely, but this does not result in internal change (Beaudoin, 2013).

Regardless of structure, administrators may desire to start with the willing (Shattuck, 2013) in order to avoid top-down directives (Beaudoin, 2013). This approach may result in inconsistent course development due to variations in enthusiasm and resistance and lack of direction. This approach could work if faculty are incentivized to address specific goals. Revenue-sharing models in which distance education units partner with academic departments and share tuition profits can be effective in increasing online degree programs (Casiello & Huling, 2013). This approach encourages the willing and those without strong views in favor or against.

Analysis and Reflection.   The following questions can help administrators analyze existing structures, areas of overlap, use of resources, and new possibilities. Institutional vision for distance learning should guide this process. An appropriate organizational structure leads to effective and sustainable distance learning operations that support institutional goals.

- How do proposed initiatives fit the current structure? Is the structure centralized or decentralized? Which will best help the institution attain its goals?
- Does the institution have a designated unit or multiple units charged with the development, delivery, and support of distance education programs? How effective is this?
- If multiple units are involved, are responsibilities clear, do units coordinate well, do responsibilities overlap, and do faculty understand differences across the areas and know where to get support? How would restructuring reduce or eliminate competition or misunderstandings or allow for resources to be better aligned?
- What pieces are missing or misaligned that might affect the success of distance education initiatives?
- What are the philosophies of staff in the distance education unit or associated areas? Do leaders of these units have a clear vision? Are these aligned with the institutional vision? How can a vision be formed and articulated?

Micro- or Project-Level Structures

Project management includes oversight for curriculum (faculty involvement, workload, course development priorities, design, quality); staffing (project manager, instructional designer, technology specialist, academic adviser, marketing coordinator); faculty effectiveness (pedagogical and technology training, student ratings); assessment (student learning outcomes); technology (learning management systems, delivery tools); and logistics (procedures for registering and enrolling students, financial aid) (Kearsley, 2013). Organizational approaches at the micro level must be designed to effectively support these functions. The following discussion assists administrators in identifying and addressing gaps between existing and optimal structures, and examines roles and responsibilities in project development.

Figure 3.1. Team-Based Design Model

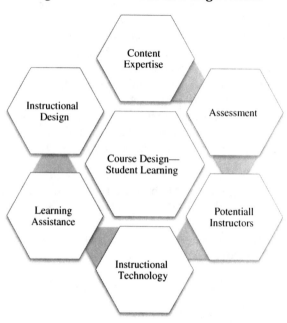

Team-Based.   Distance course development generally requires a team of experts. Even when faculty members design their own courses, they may consult with colleagues, instructional designers, technology experts, librarians, and assessment specialists. In many institutions, instructional designers and related resources are available in distance education units and provide design, curriculum, and technology assistance. Rather than one-on-one consultations with various experts, however, a team-based design model involves all those who will impact learning (UNLV Faculty Institute on Research-Based Learning for High Impact Classes, 2010).

Figure 3.1 identifies possible individuals or units in a team-based model. Instead of the student contacting various individuals or areas for help while enrolled, this support is incorporated into the course initially. Team members have specific roles. The assessment specialist could provide diagnostic testing, unit mastery measures, assignment rubrics and related training, and final assessments. The librarian might develop research materials. The technology expert could guide instructional technology selection and create learning management system tutorials. Learning assistance staff could write and teach units on in-text citations, reference lists, and study strategies, or give assignment feedback based on rubrics developed by the assessment specialist. Peer tutors might facilitate online study sessions or meet with students in real-time appointments. An instructional designer

New Directions for Higher Education • DOI: 10.1002/he

Table 3.1. Micro-Level Analysis

Model	Summary	Considerations
Team-Based	A learner-centered model involving individuals from across the institution who contribute to course design and teaching. Teams can be limited to members of a department who draw on outside expertise as needed.	What are the advantages and disadvantages of a team-based model? What is needed in terms of support, expertise, and resources? Who should be involved? How can this model be sustained? What are the advantages and disadvantages of limiting the team to the department level?
Project Oversight	An advisory committee provides vision, strategic planning, resources, and support. A project manager or coordinator addresses project logistics and day-to-day operations.	How can an advisory board ensure the success of a project? What is its role? Who should be appointed? What are the responsibilities of the project manager, and who should be appointed?

learning as the means to increase access, address space limitations, manage growth, expand enrollment, provide flexibility, accelerate degree completion, or generate revenue. Faculty may wish to use new technology to improve learning or modify their courses for online delivery, or be opposed to online coursework. They may lack information about institutional vision, while administrators may be unfamiliar with curriculum constraints, amount of time required for development, desired learning outcomes, resource needs, and learner/teacher support issues.

Although the majority of chief academic officers feel that the quality of distance education programs is equal to their face-to-face equivalents, they observe that faculty members are less convinced (Allen & Seaman, 2013). Administrators must consider differing views and how to address them. An initial step is to examine the internal and external environments in which the distance learning initiative is situated and the roles and interests of stakeholders. The goal is to agree on a vision. Identifying internal and external stakeholders, their vision, motivations, and levels of commitment, support, or opposition will help administrators anticipate possible challenges in building positive, collaborative relationships. This awareness is valuable at broad, institutional levels as well as the project management level.

Participatory Cultures. Institutions of higher education are loosely structured with no centralized power, considerable independent behavior, strong faculty autonomy, and sometimes informal or unclear reporting lines (Andrade, 2011). Academic departments are organized around disciplinary knowledge in colleges or professional schools. The curriculum is the purview of the faculty, which has ownership of content, delivery, and pedagogy. Support areas such as libraries, learning assistance, informational technology, and faculty centers may not be directly connected to academic departments. These loosely coupled structures do not encourage collaboration.

Building community among stakeholders can be addressed by considering participatory or web culture models (Bass, 2012; Jenkins, Purushotma, Clinton, Weigel, & Robison, 2006). These cultures connect individuals with shared areas of expertise and interest, and feature "low barriers to entry, strong support for sharing one's contributions, informal mentorship … , a sense of connection to each other, [and] a sense of ownership in what is being created" (Bass, 2012, p. 27). In contrast, traditional committees, which may oversee established processes or create new initiatives, can be characterized by competing interests, diverse agendas, lack of interest, and differing reporting lines. Even though a formal group may exist, it may not constitute a community in the sense of shared expertise, collective vision, common goals, mentorship, and collaboration. Thus, an environment must be created in which these characteristics can be nurtured. The leadership strategies next discussed provide suggestions.

Leadership Principles

"Institutions that will lead distance education in the future will not address the changing realities of education from a reactive perspective" (Watkins, Kaufman, & Odunlami, 2013, p. 462). Leaders must understand the difference between strategies for change creation and for change management, and which approach is most appropriate. Examples might include being proactive as opposed to being reactive, leading rather than following, and taking a long-term approach instead of making short-term fixes (Watkins et al., 2013).

Although research on leadership specific to distance education is not well developed (Beaudoin, 2013), general leadership theories and principles apply. Elements of situational leadership to examine readiness for change, and transformative leadership to adapt to change, can encourage institutions and their constituents to recognize the benefits of distance education (Beaudoin, 2013). This section reviews leadership principles for initiating and managing the change that often accompanies distance education in order to "create conditions conducive to energy, initiative, and innovation" (p. 474).

Change Initiation and Management.   Individuals must understand the rationale for change and believe it will be beneficial before they will support it; ideally, change should be co-created (Wheatley, 2005). Often a new idea appears as simply different, but not better. Claims that the change will produce certain results may be supposition. Regarding distance learning, leaders must avoid finding an educational problem wanting a solution in the form of new technology (Watkins et al., 2013). "Distance education is a means not an end" (p. 455) and should be implemented to achieve specific results.

Few will accept a case for change without compelling evidence of need (Eckel, Green, Hill, & Mallon, 1999). If institutions "fail to systematically and scientifically explore whether they have good reasons to create a distance education program" (Watkins et al., 2013, p. 453), this will soon be apparent. For change to be successful, need and vision must be clear, and a commitment to involving and empowering stakeholders to co-create it must be apparent. Only then will change be permanent, although it will still likely be incremental.

Strategies. Bolman and Deal (2008) advocate reframing, or examining situations through four lenses—structural, human resource, political, and symbolic. The human resource frame examines the impact of change on individuals. Fear and insecurity are typical reactions. Faculty members may feel their positions are threatened, their contributions are undervalued, and they lack needed expertise. They may criticize the quality or effectiveness of distance delivery. To address this, leaders must provide resources and opportunities for training and support. Those who feel unsettled by distance learning can be given opportunities to contribute in areas in which they have knowledge and expertise such as writing, editing, or research.

Acknowledgment of a job well done is also critical and the focus of the symbolic frame. Leaders can reward effort through stipends, public recognition, awards, events, celebrations, opportunities to showcase achievements, and professional development. Support for project-related presentations and research is valuable for those seeking tenure or rank advancement. While some individuals are intrinsically motivated and satisfied by their own sense of accomplishment (Shattuck, 2013), having achievements acknowledged builds future support.

Considering the political frame is an important aspect of leading change. Diverse teams have greater potential for innovation than those consisting of like-minded individuals, but reaching consensus may be difficult. The key to understanding various perspectives is to be open, understanding, and respectful. Stakeholders must work to resolve differences rather than ignoring them, and be willing to negotiate and compromise. Opportunities for discussion, airing viewpoints, and exploration are needed to find common ground.

Another leadership approach is based on the idea that resisting change is more typical than embracing it. Successful change involves three considerations—why (reason), what or how much (substance), and who and how (process) (Eckel et al., 1999). Stakeholders must believe that the status quo is unsatisfactory and that change is beneficial (*reason*). The *substance* of the change involves examining the pressure to change and its extent (e.g., a minor modification affecting limited areas, or an extensive, program-wide or institution-wide transformation). The third element focuses on whom to involve (*process*). This necessitates designing appropriate structures, providing opportunities for debate and exploration, and negotiating campus culture. Finally, evaluation of the change must occur to determine if it has been effective.

Wheatley (2005) suggests that effective organizational change must be based on the "assumption that people, like all life, are creative and good at change" (p. 76). She offers four principles: (1) involve people in creating change; (2) understand that people react to directives rather than obeying them, so leaders should not expect obedience to a plan; (3) recognize that people see and interpret reality differently; and (4) assume that organizations possess the expertise needed to determine new directions and to implement change; the role of the leader is to provide connections across the organization to stimulate "the creation of new information" (p. 93). Wheatley emphasizes the human spirit, the freedom to create, and appropriate structures to support this.

Finally, Kotter's (2005) eight-step process for change—creating a sense of urgency, pulling together a guiding team, developing vision and strategy, communicating for understanding and buy-in, empowering others, producing short-term gains, not letting up, and creating a new culture—shares similarities with the previous approaches. Kotter emphasizes using compelling stories based on actual experiences to change how people feel. This approach emphasizes the why and how elements of change and suggests a strong leadership role. In cases in which urgency is not readily apparent, Kotter advocates for conveying a sense of urgency to help move change forward.

Analysis and Reflection.   Commonalities among the approaches are evident. These include communicating need, establishing structures that enable connections and creativity, and co-creating vision. The following questions, adapted from Eckel et al. (1999), guide an analysis of change.

- Why does the institution need to change direction? What are the consequences if it does not? What steps can be taken to increase awareness of the need?
- Will changes in approach result in an improvement for programs, students, and the institution? How will this change improve teaching and learning?
- How do different individuals or groups perceive the proposed change? How critical is it to manage these differing perceptions? How can this be done?
- What are possible reasons for resistance? What might specific individuals have to give up due to the change? What strategies can be implemented to gain their support?

Conclusion

This chapter has identified structural and leadership issues pertinent to distance learning. Organizational structures at macro and micro levels must be examined to ensure that they are designed to accomplish institutional vision. This involves considering the effectiveness of existing systems, and how to work within them, change them, or develop new structures. Those initiating or leading projects must identify the stakeholders, their goals or agendas, individuals who can contribute, and how to manage differing perspectives or visions.

Successful projects are collaborative. Negotiation may be needed in terms of diverse perspectives to achieve goals. Finally, understanding human nature as it relates to change and identifying appropriate strategies are critical in establishing the needed foundation for successful distance learning initiatives.

References

Allen, I. E., & Seaman, J. (2013). *Changing course: Ten years of tracking online education in the United States.* Babson Park, MA: Babson Survey Research Group and Quahog Research Group. Retrieved from http://sloanconsortium.org/publications/survey/changing_course_2012

Andrade, M. S. (2011). Managing change—engaging faculty in assessment opportunities. *Innovative Higher Education, 36*(4), 217–233.

Andrade, M. S. (2013). Global learning by distance: Principles and practicalities for learner support. *International Journal of Online Pedagogy and Course Design, 3*(1), 66–81.

Bass, R. (2012). Disrupting ourselves: The problems of learning in higher education. *EDUCAUSE Review, 47*(2), 23–33.

Beaudoin, M. (2013). Institutional leadership. In M. G. Moore (Ed.), *Handbook of distance education* (3rd ed., pp. 467–480). New York: Routledge.

Bolman, L. G., & Deal, T. E. (2008). *Reframing organizations: Artistry, choice, and leadership.* San Francisco, CA: John Wiley & Sons.

Casiello, A. R., & Huling, H. (2013, August). *Revenue sharing as an incentive to online program expansion.* Paper presented at the 29th Annual Conference on Distance Teaching & Learning, Madison, WI.

Eckel, P., Green, M., Hill, B., & Mallon, W. (1999). *On change III: Taking charge of change: A primer for colleges and universities.* Washington, DC: American Council on Education. Retrieved from http://www.acenet.edu/bookstore/pdf/on-change/on-changeIII.pdf

Eskey, M. T. (2010). *Distance education: The centralization vs. decentralization debate.* Retrieved from http://www.facultyfocus.com/articles/distance-learning/distance-education-the-centralization-vs-decentralization-debate/

Jenkins, H., Purushotma, R., Clinton, K., Weigel, M., & Robison, A. J. (2006). *Confronting the challenges of participatory culture: Media education for the 21st century.* John D. and Catherine T. MacArthur Foundation. Retrieved from http://www.newmedialiteracies.org/files/working/NMLWhitePaper.pdf

Kearsley, G. (2013). Management of online programs. In M. G. Moore (Ed.), *Handbook of distance education* (3rd ed., pp. 425–436). New York: Routledge.

Kotter, J. (2005). *Our iceberg is melting: Changing and succeeding under any conditions.* New York: St. Martin's Press.

Shattuck, K. (2013). Faculty participation in online distance education. In M. G. Moore (Ed.), *Handbook of distance education* (3rd ed., pp. 390–402). New York: Routledge.

UNLV Faculty Institute on Research-Based Learning for High Impact Classes. (2010). Retrieved from http://www.library.unlv.edu/faculty/institute/

Watkins, R., Kaufman, R., & Odunlami, B. (2013). Strategic planning and needs assessment in distance education. In M. G. Moore (Ed.), *Handbook of distance education* (3rd ed., pp. 452–466). New York: Routledge.

Wheatley, M. J. (2005). *Finding our way: Leadership for an uncertain time.* San Francisco, CA: Berrett-Koehler.

White, C. (2005). Towards a learner-based theory of distance language learning: The concept of the learner-context interface. In B. Holmberg, M. Shelley, & C. White (Eds.), *Distance education and languages: Evolution and change* (pp. 55–71). Clevedon, UK: Multilingual Matters.

MAUREEN SNOW ANDRADE *is associate vice president of Academic Affairs for Academic Programs at Utah Valley University. Her responsibilities include distance learning, faculty development, assessment, curriculum development, degree completion, general education, and graduate studies.*

NEW DIRECTIONS FOR HIGHER EDUCATION • DOI: 10.1002/he

4

A key step in distance learning project management is the creation of a course development plan. The plan should account for decisions related to materials, curriculum, delivery methods, staffing, technology applications, resources, reporting lines, and project management—issues that may require administrator involvement and support, particularly for evolving distance learning programs.

The Course Development Plan: Macro-Level Decisions and Micro-Level Processes

Karen Franker, Dennis James

A crucial consideration in distance education planning is how to create policies, support structures, and processes that ensure the development of world-class online courses that incorporate the highest standards for teaching and learning. An exemplary course development model provides a common framework for consistency, design, pedagogy, and content that aligns with educational mission and institutional vision (Puzziferro & Shelton, 2008). This model should also incorporate a scalable plan to provide a sufficient number of courses to attract students to course offerings (Oblinger & Hawkins, 2006).

Although institutions may vary in the structure, administration, and funding of their distance education programs, the key decisions related to course content, delivery mode, technology, and project management are common to all. This chapter first examines the critical macro-level conversations regarding institutional planning, communication strategies, support structures, and policy decisions that underpin the development of rigorous, responsive, and cohesive online courses. Next, it identifies the essential micro-level components in designing a holistic course development process that incorporates shared expertise, project management, course quality standards, universal design, and continuous improvement to ensure consistently successful courses.

NEW DIRECTIONS FOR HIGHER EDUCATION, no. 173, Spring 2016 © 2016 Wiley Periodicals, Inc.
Published online in Wiley Online Library (wileyonlinelibrary.com) • DOI: 10.1002/he.20178

Creating an Institutional Course Development Plan

A course development plan provides a comprehensive framework for the administrative decisions that support the implementation of distance education courses. The following sections describe specific institutional planning, communication strategies, and support structures for distance education leaders to consider when creating a plan.

Institutional Planning.   The first step in creating a course development plan is to determine the goals and philosophy of course development in relation to the institutional plan for developing and assessing on-ground courses. A statement of overarching course design principles is commonly part of the curriculum development portion of a distance education business plan and may include course quality standards and their alignment with academic or strategic plans. The business plan provides a foundation for course design efficiency, productivity, and scalability for the entire institution (Puzziferro & Shelton, 2008). Even in institutions where online course development is decentralized at a department or school level, it is important to have institution-wide standards for consistency in course objectives, course organization, and syllabus design.

The course development portion of the business plan contains an overview of staffing and financial resources to support course development. This may include faculty stipends and per-course costs for instructional design and multimedia, as well as projected course revision cycles, job titles, and full-time equivalents (FTE) for all staff positions related to course development.

Communication Strategies.   Quality online programs represent a partnership of (a) technical and administrative personnel, (b) instructional designers and faculty, and (c) decision makers who allocate fiscal and human resources (MacDonald & Thompson, 2005). In Chapter 3 of this volume, Maureen Snow Andrade makes the point that distance learning is becoming increasingly mainstream in higher education. In order to gain widespread acceptance and understanding, it is essential that college leaders advocate for a jointly developed course development plan as an iterative process with critical campus stakeholders such as faculty, academic deans, information technology (IT) staff, and the senior leadership team.

Knowing that it takes a coordinated effort to create and sustain successful online courses, decision makers must communicate a shared and consistent vision of how instructional design processes can help the institution achieve its educational mission (Vasser, 2010). Since the rationale for effective instructional design practices may be unfamiliar to stakeholders, leaders must be clear in their own minds about the value of creating pedagogically and technically sound online courses before communicating those concepts to others.

Support Structures.   Course development planning conversations may take months to move through various groups, and will benefit from

New Directions for Higher Education • DOI: 10.1002/he

the leadership of a director or dean of distance education who reports directly to a provost or vice president for academic affairs.

In addition, the formation of an ongoing campus-wide distance education advisory committee enables input from a variety of campus stakeholders to ensure the inclusion of multiple perspectives. While the committee might not make formal decisions, it can serve as a sounding board for assessing distance education policies and practices. Members of an advisory committee might include the director of information technology, a campus dean, the director of distance education, a student, faculty members, a financial officer, a librarian, a disabilities director, and a marketing director.

Policy Decisions.   With a leadership structure in place, the planning process for the development of online courses can move forward with critical academic, business, and technology decisions that influence the allocation of financial and human resources. Institutions must consider where the final approval should reside for each type of decision, as this will affect which office to consult.

All decision-making processes should be transparent and clearly understood by stakeholders. For example, does the authority for determining which courses to offer online rest within a central distance education unit or within a department or program, and what are the advantages of each? Also, which office will be responsible for hiring and evaluating online faculty—a human resources office, a dean, or a central distance education unit? The appropriate responses will vary from campus to campus, but developing clarity around decision-making authority ensures efficient resolution of any issues that arise.

What follow are listings of the primary academic, business, and information technology policy and planning decisions to consider when setting up a course development plan, many of which carry financial implications. Explanatory comments follow each list of questions. Vasser (2010) states that lists of this type are by no means completely inclusive, but indicate the general types of advance planning needed for a smooth rollout of distance education courses.

Academic Policy Decisions.

- How will the registrar designate course delivery formats in the course schedule (e.g., fully online, predominantly online, blended online)? Will all students have the option of taking both on-ground and online courses (Vasser, 2010)?
- Will all online courses and key assessments align with the existing program curriculum through a curriculum map or other framework?
- How will the institution ensure quality and academic integrity in its online courses?
- How will faculty members receive training and support for designing and delivering online courses?

Course delivery definitions. If course delivery will incorporate a variety of formats, how will the institution differentiate between them in the timetable or course catalog so that students, faculty, and staff are clear about delivery methods and face-to-face meeting requirements? This is important for scheduling classrooms and for helping students and advisers to understand the time commitment and course formats that match individual learning styles. Each institution will have unique course delivery designators, depending on program needs, and persons involved in this decision are typically the registrar, deans, and program directors. The following are sample designators for undergraduate and graduate distance education courses at Edgewood College:

- Fully online: 100% of the course is delivered online; there are no required face-to-face sessions.
- Predominantly online: 80% or more of the course is delivered online, with the remaining 20% or less delivered in one or two required face-to-face sessions.
- Blended online: 40% or more of the course is delivered online, with the remaining portion delivered in required face-to-face sessions. Faculty members determine the length and frequency of face-to-face sessions, as long as they do not exceed 60% of the course.

Curriculum mapping and assessment plan. In the planning of online courses, it is essential to determine how courses will mesh with existing curriculum in terms of learning outcomes and assessments. When designing a fully online program, it is useful to develop a map or matrix of learning outcomes and key assessments for each course. Such a map may not currently exist for on-ground courses, but is helpful in providing a big picture view of the curricular structure of each program as well as invaluable guidance for the online design team. In addition, mapping facilitates using course outcomes as the starting point of course design in accordance with backward design principles (Wiggins & McTighe, 2005).

A typical curriculum map lists the desired program outcomes and key assessments along the left side of a matrix; then, within cells below the appropriate course numbers it notes where the administration of each assessment resides. This ensures minimal overlap in course content and assessments within a program, and provides a clear picture of how each course fits into the overall framework. Curriculum mapping typically involves the appropriate dean, program director, and lead faculty, as well as a member of the central online team.

Course quality standards. A common faculty concern is that online courses are less academically rigorous and of lower quality than on-ground offerings (Allen & Seaman, 2012; Wickersham & McElhany, 2010). To address this concern, many institutions utilize a course quality rubric. One example is the Quality Matters (QM) Rubric™ (Quality Matters, 2014) that provides a research-based framework for assessing course design quality for online and blended courses. Some institutions choose to develop their own rubrics based on input from faculty and staff. No matter which rubric an institution adopts, the underlying importance is to adhere to quality measures of effective course design. An additional faculty concern is upholding academic integrity, which may involve student identity verification or proctoring of online exams.

Faculty training, support, and collaboration. Central to the planning of effective courses is the awareness that developing and delivering them require pedagogical and technical expertise that may not currently exist among faculty at a particular institution (Oblinger & Hawkins, 2006). Faculty members tend to be primarily subject matter experts (SMEs), and generally do not receive formal training in effective pedagogy or technology use as part of their professional preparation. Thus, a major task is how to provide support in writing effective learning objectives, designing formative online assessments, and developing assignments that fit the online environment. Instructors also need technical support in using the learning management system (LMS) and course tools such as wikis and blogs (Oblinger & Hawkins, 2006). Training, both formal and informal, is an essential part of the effort to familiarize faculty with the processes and pedagogical methods involved in developing online courses.

Last, institutions with a strong concern for providing high-quality learning experiences have found that a "Lone Ranger" approach to course development does not scale well, and that the most effective online courses represent collaborative teamwork that incorporates the shared expertise of instructors and course development teams (Oblinger & Hawkins, 2006). In these partnerships, the faculty member is the SME, with the instructional design team providing expertise in learning theory and course design strategies. A challenge of this collaborative model is the required mental shift for faculty to be open to co-creation of courses that incorporate active learning strategies, and to re-envision their faculty role as facilitators of learning rather than transmitters of knowledge.

Business Policy Decisions.

- What are the institution's policies on course ownership, faculty compensation, and copyright as they pertain to online courses?
- Will instructional design services be in-house or outsourced to a third-party vendor?

Course ownership, faculty compensation, and copyright. A common legal issue is determining ownership of distance learning course content (Twigg, 2000). In contrast to a traditional course that may only have a printed syllabus and exams, the content of an online course is largely contained within a learning management system. Both faculty members and institutions often wish to retain rights to online course content. The institution may wish to reuse the content in future course offerings, whereas the faculty member may view the material as proprietary content that is owned by the person who created it, to be used as that individual sees fit.

There is merit in both positions; however, to avoid confusion it is important for an institution to clarify its intellectual property and online course development policies, and to clearly communicate them before course design begins. Also, policies that serve the middle ground between institutional and faculty interests tend to receive the greatest acceptance. This may include arrangements in which the institution shares after-expense profits with faculty, with the exact split negotiated before courses run (Twigg, 2000).

Many colleges pay instructors a stipend to develop an online course, and require them to sign a course development contract as a work-for-hire agreement with the institution. In many cases, a college devotes considerable staffing resources toward the development of online courses, including instructional designers and multimedia experts, and wishes to ensure a return on its investment (Kranch, 2008). The course development contract specifies deadlines and payments for course completion, as well as language regarding present and future uses of course content by both the instructor and the institution. This amount of detail may seem excessive, but serves to clarify ownership and avoid misinterpretations.

In addition to ownership and intellectual property, another legal issue is developing policies for copyright and fair use of course materials. Courses offered at a distance typically reside in a central digital location, and violations of copyright are more likely to occur due to the ease of scanning, copying, pasting, and reusing content. An institution's librarians can serve as valuable partners in assisting faculty and staff with correct use of digital materials in online course sites.

Outsourcing versus in-house development. An important institutional business decision is the determination of who will develop online courses. Although the majority of colleges decide to develop courses in-house (Clinefelter & Magda, 2013), an alternative option is to purchase instructional design services from a third-party vendor. This often provides a quicker way to ramp up initial course development for new online programs without a substantial investment in staffing. Although there is no one-size-fits-all answer, a decision on outsourcing has implications for the types of financial and human resources required for course development and thus requires careful consideration from many perspectives.

Technology Decisions.

- Which LMS will house courses (e.g., Moodle, Blackboard, Desire2Learn)? Will server administration be in-house or through a vendor?
- Which software tools and equipment are essential in supporting course development (e.g., screen-casting, speech-to-text software, web

conferencing tools, project management tools, collaboration tools, and video equipment)?

- Which administrative roles and permissions will the course development team need to access, build, and revise courses within the LMS and other instructional technology tools such as e-portfolio systems?
- Which staff and units will provide support and server hosting for online course technology?

Selection of an LMS. An LMS serves as a container and virtual classroom space for online course content and provides a password-protected environment for course access. LMS tools facilitate collaboration and provide secure access to quizzes and grades. Selecting an LMS requires input from key campus stakeholders such as the director of information technology, the academic technologist, faculty, distance learning team, the registrar, and deans. This diverse group membership ensures that the LMS fulfills a broad range of user needs and perspectives.

Selection and purchase of technology tools. Specialized technology tools commonly used by faculty and instructional designers in developing and teaching online courses include screen-casting software for tutorial creation; graphic design software to create and edit images; web design software to create course style sheets; and web conferencing tools to provide real-time video collaboration for course design teams, faculty, and students. In addition, institutions should consider tools that caption videos and convert speech to text.

Software access permissions for course development team. All team members will access courses in the LMS and in password-protected software such as e-portfolio systems. Often access will need to be at a course designer or administrator level to have the full range of editing capabilities. A central IT staff member usually handles these permissions.

Technology support and hosting. Another key technology decision is to determine the level and type of technology support to provide for online courses. Will technology support and hosting of the LMS be an in-house or a third-party arrangement? The advantages of in-house hosting include greater control over scheduling server maintenance and downtime; however, colleges with limited technology staffing might find it more efficient to have vendor-performed maintenance. An additional decision is whether to extend help desk availability beyond normal business hours to accommodate the schedules of online learners. While very few college help desks offer round-the-clock availability, a significant number offer extended evening and weekend hours.

Designing and Implementing a Course Development Process

Once key macro-level decisions are in place, leaders can move on to micro-level processes related to course creation, project management, quality assurance, universal design, and continuous course improvement. When mindfully organized into a cohesive whole, these processes result in high-quality courses completed on schedule. This section describes the steps in developing essential micro-level processes to support overall course development.

A first step in process planning is assembling and coordinating a capable team. Course design should be a collaborative process where the former model of faculty working in isolated silos shifts to one of faculty working together with specialists to ensure that courses meet the needs of students and accrediting bodies (Vasser, 2010). Since instructors often lack the technical expertise to capture the power of the learning management system or to deal with its idiosyncrasies, a team approach allows them to focus on developing exemplary content rather than getting bogged down in technical details.

Once the institution designates a team, a second step in process planning is to have the team create a clear and consistent process for designing courses. Molenda (2010) asserts the importance of structured instructional design processes to provide the highest-quality course development. These processes commonly include a course development guide and course design document that lay out recommended features to include in all courses, such as objectives, activities, assessments, and multimedia requirements. This guide serves as a road map in structuring the entire course, module by module and as a whole. While course design can be sequential, it is necessary to frequently revisit the design document to pose new questions, clarify expectations, and revise content. Misaligned activities and assessments can cause the course to lose structural and pedagogical integrity.

By having a consistent format for instructional designers and faculty to follow, course creation is more effective, efficient, and economical. The keys to a successful process are: (a) cohesive and holistic design, (b) solid project management, (c) course quality standards, (d) universal accessibility and usability design practices, and (e) the cultivation of a continuous improvement culture.

Cohesive and Holistic Course Creation.   Holistic means *all, whole, entire,* or *total.* Holism is the idea that systems and their properties are an integrated whole rather than a collection of separate parts. In course design, from face-to-face settings all the way to 100% online, the process is often broken into components without regard for the interactions between them. This can cause miscommunication between an instructional designer, academic technologist, media developer, and faculty member, which can translate into confusion for the student in the form of scattered and confusing course design. A collaborative approach to course development allows for a cohesive, rigorous, and responsive course design process that is adaptable to most teaching strategies or philosophies, and improves the ability to achieve higher course quality standards (Chao, Saj, & Hamilton, 2010).

When courses are in development, the instructional design team works closely with each department or program to design templates that take the

Figure 4.1. Course Template Layout

Getting Started	Welcome	• First Steps in the Class • Course Navigation Guide (Graphic and Video)
	Syllabus	• Instructor Contact Information • Required Materials • PDF Version
In the Classroom	Announcements	
	Modules	• Weekly Objectives • Weekly Checklist (to help students plan their week) • Required Reading and Media • Assignments
	Discussions	
	Web Tools	
Your Progress	Grades	
	Portfolio	
Support	College Services	• Technical Assistance • Library Services • Student Support Services
	LMS Help	

guesswork out of course design structure, add consistency to the student experience, and allow faculty to focus on course activities, interactions, and assessments. With solid templates in place, instructional designers can concentrate on technology solutions that work with the curriculum, rather than making a "cool" technology tool fit course outcomes. Figure 4.1 illustrates a common course template layout, with items in the left column representing navigation buttons, and items in the other two columns representing pages that open after a user clicks on a button.

Project Management.   In addition to having a cohesive team and solid design process in place, online course development requires a support structure that incorporates sound project management techniques, including the central scheduling and tracking of course design projects and deadlines. An instructional design manager oversees issues related to technology, instructional designers, staff, and faculty, and ensures that effective communication processes are in place for team members to update progress on projects. This may include a central repository of course design documents accessible to all team members.

Course Quality Standards.   All courses benefit from a rigorous checklist that incorporates the following standards: user access to content regardless of web browser or operating system; attention to accessibility requirements, ensuring an equivalent user experience for people with disabilities; student access to campus services; opportunities for instructor-to-student and student-to-student interactions; and written standards for instructor-to-student communication. As previously mentioned, a course quality rubric provides a framework for quality assurance throughout all aspects of course design.

Two other components for ensuring quality are a syllabus with directions that adequately prepare the learner, and performance expectations based on learning outcomes. Syllabus headings might include: Course Organization, Course Objectives, Classroom Code of Conduct, General Grading Policies, Rubrics for Discussion Posting, and Assignments. Link checking and proofreading are additional final quality checks before a course site opens to students.

Universal Design.   As applied to online courses, universal design incorporates the mind-set that institutions should not wait for students to ask for a disability accommodation before considering how to provide one. When universal design becomes an integral part of course design, institutions are taking a proactive approach to improved learning and access for all students. This includes the following principles: An equivalent user experience is provided for students with disabilities; usability results in a course that is effective, efficient, and satisfying; and usable accessibility provides a positive user experience, not only for people with disabilities, but for all students (Center for Applied Special Technology, 2012).

Continuous Course Improvement.   In addition to accessibility considerations, an effective course design process supports a culture of continuous improvement that incorporates new technologies, updated content, and revised assessments. At the end of a course, an instructional designer should meet with the instructor to discuss future revisions. An improvement plan details revised course goals, success measures, and supporting tasks, including review of overall student performance. In addition, it incorporates questions that students have raised about assignments or assessments, an analysis of course evaluations, technology issues, and the instructor's perceptions of the overall course flow and structure.

When course improvements are made incrementally and continually rather than at widely spaced set intervals, faculty and instructional designers can be more creative in their improvements as they have a longer time line to effect changes between course offerings rather than a "just in time, just enough" approach. This results in courses that are constantly refreshed, relevant, current, and engaging for students and faculty.

Conclusion

Quality online course development occurs as the result of collaborative, organized, and informed decision making that incorporates the perspectives of a variety of campus stakeholders. An institution's commitment to world-class courses is evident in smoothly coordinated, holistic design processes that are responsive to the changing needs of students and faculty while embracing recognized standards for effective learning design. Administrators charged with the development of successful distance learning courses understand that the investment in forging collaborative relationships and frequent communications with campus stakeholders pays off in increased student and faculty satisfaction with the total online education experience.

References

Allen, I. E., & Seaman, J. (2012). *Conflicted: Faculty and online education, 2012.* Babson Park, MA: Babson Survey Research Group. Retrieved from http://www .insidehighered.com/sites/default/server_files/survey/conflicted.html

Center for Applied Special Technology. (2012). *UDL guidelines—version 2.0: Examples and resources.* Retrieved from http://www.udlcenter.org/implementation/examples

Chao, I. T., Saj, T., & Hamilton, D. (2010). Using collaborative course development to achieve online course quality standards. *International Review of Research in Open & Distance Learning, 11*(3), 110–112.

Clinefelter, D. L., & Magda, A. J. (2013). *Online learning at private colleges and universities: A survey of chief academic officers.* Louisville, KY: Learning House.

Kranch, D. A. (2008). Who owns online course intellectual property? *Quarterly Review of Distance Education, 9*(4), 349–356, 445.

MacDonald, C. J., & Thompson, T. L. (2005). Structure, content, delivery, service, and outcomes: Quality e-learning in higher education. *International Review of Research in Open & Distance Learning, 6*(2), 19.

Molenda, M. (2010). Origins and evolution of instructional systems design. In *Handbook of improving performance in the workplace* (Vol. 1). 53–92.

Oblinger, D. G., & Hawkins, B. L. (2006). The myth about online course development: A faculty member can individually develop and deliver an effective online course. *EDUCAUSE Review, 41*(1), 14–15.

Puzziferro, M., & Shelton, K. (2008). A model for developing high-quality online courses: Integrating a systems approach with learning theory. *Journal of Asynchronous Learning Networks, 12*(3–4). Retrieved from http://sloanconsortium.org/jaln/v12n3 /model-developing-high-quality-online-courses-integrating-systems-approach-learni ng-theory

Quality Matters. (2014). Higher education rubric, 5th Edition. Retrieved from http://www.qualitymatters.org/rubric

Twigg, C. A. (2000). Who owns online courses and course materials? Intellectual property policies for a new learning environment. Retrieved from http://www.thencat.org /Monographs/Mono2.pdf

Vasser, N. (2010). Instructional design processes and traditional colleges. *Online Journal of Distance Learning Administration, 13*(4). Retrieved from http://www.westga.edu /~distance/ojdla/winter134/vasser134.html

Wickersham, L. E., & McElhany, J. A. (2010). Bridging the divide: Reconciling administrator and faculty concerns regarding online education. *Quarterly Review of Distance Education, 11*(1), 1–12, 60–61.

Wiggins, G. P., & McTighe, J. (2005). *Understanding by design* (3rd ed.). Alexandria, VA: ASCD.

KAREN FRANKER *is the director of online learning at Edgewood College in Madison, Wisconsin.*

DENNIS JAMES *is the online course development manager at Edgewood College in Madison, Wisconsin.*

5

This chapter explores how course designers and content writers engage with each other, develop materials, and determine a design model, course components, and supporting technology.

Writing Materials: Insights Into Course Design and Writing Processes

Aubrey Olsen Bronson

Motivation for creating online courses comes from various sources. At the institutional level, two common reasons for launching online programs are increasing access for off-campus students and improving quality for on-campus students (Miller & Schiffman, 2006). Particularly for courses traditionally taught in large auditoriums, conversion to hybrid or online delivery allows institutions to not only reach a larger number of students but also enhance overall course quality. These improvements may come in the form of greater flexibility, increased interaction, or access to additional resources not available in the traditional setting. For individual faculty members, motivation may come from pedagogical advantages, personal or professional growth, or a chance to earn additional income (Allen & Seaman, 2008).

Whatever the motivation, developing a new online course is a multifaceted undertaking. Understanding the course design process can assist decision makers in supporting faculty members as they develop new courses. Familiarity with the micro level of design can also help administrators ensure that online materials result in quality courses that promote opportunities for active and engaged learning.

Process

Materials writing for distance course development requires a surprising amount of time. It can take several semesters to launch a single course. Figure 5.1 outlines a possible sequence for the development of a new course. Each step in the process—planning, building, piloting, revising, and launching—often takes an entire semester. Because technological resources and options have increased, "more time is required for the different stages of course planning, design, development and evaluation. This is still

NEW DIRECTIONS FOR HIGHER EDUCATION, no. 173, Spring 2016 © 2016 Wiley Periodicals, Inc.
Published online in Wiley Online Library (wileyonlinelibrary.com) • DOI: 10.1002/he.20179

Figure 5.1. Course Development Time Line

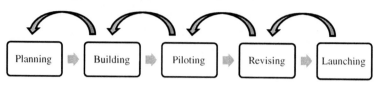

often underestimated by novice distance ... teachers and by management" (White, 2003, p. 73). To build a quality course, sufficient time is needed in each stage, and even after one phase is completed, issues encountered in the next stage may require designers to step back, rethink, and rebuild.

Planning.   In the planning stage, subject matter experts work together to identify objectives and outcomes for the course. They make decisions about course materials, and design a scope and sequence or course planning document. Ko and Rossen (2010) suggest including course objectives, weekly units, types of interaction and activities, assignments, and exams. Figure 5.2 illustrates how a generic scope and sequence template might be organized.

An important item to consider when initiating the planning phase of the design process is whether to build the course around a textbook. A major benefit of using a textbook is faster development since less time is needed to find resources or create original materials. Not using a textbook allows developers more freedom and flexibility, but also takes more time. Another factor is cost. Using a textbook saves time for the development team, but it is more expensive for the students. Deciding which course materials to use requires a balance of cost, flexibility, and time.

Building.   When building a course, content writers work with instructional designers and technology experts to make the course materials appropriate for online delivery. A common instance might involve creating PowerPoint slides to present course content. The content writer creates a script to accompany the slides. Next, the instructional designer oversees an audio recording and uses appropriate technology to combine the audio

Figure 5.2. Scope and Sequence Template

	Objectives	Materials	Activities	Assignments	Exams
Week 1					
Week 2					
Week 3					
Week 4					

recording and PowerPoint slides into a compact video file. The video is then included in the course materials.

In addition to the creation of course materials, the building phase also includes designing assignments and assessment tools. With regard to quizzes and tests in credit-bearing courses, administrators may need to give special attention to validity and confidentiality. A frequently cited criticism of online learning is that assessment tools will be compromised. The building phase is an important time for security issues to be considered.

Piloting.   Once the building process is complete, the course can be piloted. In some cases, this first offering is made available for free or at a reduced rate. During the pilot course, the teacher watches for mistakes in the materials and ways to improve content delivery. Some fortunate teachers may have the pleasure of discovering a detail-conscious student who asks questions about incorrect page numbers, confusing instructions, or grammatical errors. Encouraging students to find and report these kinds of mistakes can be time well spent during the pilot course. It is wise to have either the subject matter expert or the content writer—who has been working on the development team—run the pilot course. This way, the teacher is familiar with the course design and is invested in the project. A conscientious teacher during the piloting phase paves the way to successful revising.

Revising.   After the course has been taught once, there will inevitably be opportunities for improvement. There are various ways to identify needed revisions. One option is to have the students enrolled in the pilot course complete an end-of-semester survey, which can include questions such as "What was the most frustrating part of this course?" or "What could be done to improve this course?" to elicit ideas for revision. Another option is to conduct observational research during the pilot. Observing students as they are working on an online course can be extremely enlightening. Consider the following scenario.

Several students in Japan enroll in an online English as a foreign language class through an American university. Part of the course focuses on building a larger vocabulary in English. The assignments and quizzes for this vocabulary component ask the students to match English words with their corresponding definitions. On a trip to Asia, a professor from the sponsoring university makes arrangements to observe some of these Japanese students as they work on their English assignments. During the observation, the American professor notices that if the students allow their cursors to hover over the English word, the definition automatically appears in a pop-up text box, thus negating the validity of the exercise. This simple observation reveals a major flaw in the course that may have otherwise gone unnoticed.

NEW DIRECTIONS FOR HIGHER EDUCATION • DOI: 10.1002/he

A semester for revising and editing gives course designers a chance to correct mistakes and make other changes as needed.

Launching.   Once necessary revisions have been made, a course can be launched. Launching a course may include assigning a course number, listing it in the university catalog, and agreeing on a permanent cycle for when (and by whom) it will be taught. Unlike a pilot course, which may not be numbered or included in the catalog, a launched course will often need to be approved by a university committee to move from temporary to permanent status.

At this point, an issue to consider is shelf life. How long will the newly developed course last before it needs to be updated? The shelf life for one subject area may be longer than for another. For example, an online course in science will probably need to be updated much sooner than an online course in ancient history. In any case, it is advantageous for designers to make sure long-lasting materials and activities have been built into the course before it is launched.

Time.   In the materials writing process, a key issue is time. When administrators commission new online courses, they typically want to see them developed quickly. Faculty members tend to be busy. Even those interested in online course design will want to be released from other responsibilities in order to have time to work on a development project. For administrators, it is important to remember that this type of released time will be needed not only for the planning and building phases, but also for the piloting and revising stages. In addition, faculty members will continue to need released time to teach the course in subsequent semesters. Providing faculty members with sufficient time to work through the iterative design process helps to ensure that the courses being developed will be quality courses.

Teamwork

Because of the time-consuming nature of course development, it may be tempting to assign an individual faculty member to design a distance course. While this approach may save some resources in the short term, there are many advantages to implementing team-based course design. First, in contrast to a course developed by a single designer, a course developed by a team will reflect a more generic style and therefore be applicable across sections. A team-based approach gives developers access to a strong support system of experts (Andrade, Chapter 3 of this volume). Working as a team also creates a sense of group ownership, which allows an institution greater flexibility in making assignments for who will teach each course.

When a development team is functioning efficiently, members work together to create quality materials. The following scenario illustrates how a subject matter expert and an instructional designer might each contribute to the development of a method for reporting student progress throughout a course:

> The subject matter expert has taught a speed-reading course on campus many times. She is currently in the process of developing the course for online delivery. In the face-to-face class, students track their reading speed and comprehension scores on a paper-based progress chart and submit the chart on several occasions during the semester. In a team meeting, the content writer explains that she would like to find a similar way for online students to track their speed-reading progress.
>
> Next, the subject matter expert and the instructional designer brainstorm ways to adapt the paper-based progress chart for online use. The instructional designer suggests creating an electronic form in which students can click to make check marks that will represent their reading speeds and comprehension scores. The electronic form can be submitted at several different times during the semester so that both teachers and students can track progress. Once all team members are in agreement, the instructional designer creates the progress chart, and when it is ready, the subject matter expert uploads it into the course.

In this example, the subject matter expert had successfully used a paper-based chart in the face-to-face setting, and she knew she wanted something that could accomplish the same goal in the new course. The instructional designer was familiar with the technological tools that would make that possible. He took the paper-based chart and converted it into an Adobe form so that students could simply click to make electronic check marks on their charts. This digital form allowed students to easily save and upload their charts so that they could be submitted to the teacher several times during the semester. Together, the subject matter expert and the instructional designer were able to create an effective tool to facilitate a quality learning experience.

Consider another scenario:

> After running an entrepreneurship series of guest lecturers for several semesters, a business department decides to create an online entrepreneurship class. A development team is formed and begins planning the scope and sequence for the course. The team chooses to video record all of the speakers scheduled to present in the entrepreneurship series for the coming semester. Arrangements are made with the director of media services to have student workers film the guest lecturers. As each new video is made available, the subject matter expert decides which parts of the talk are relevant for the course. Next, the instructional designer extracts the desired clips and prepares them for online use. Using the clips, the content writer works with the subject matter expert to develop assignments and discussion topics related to the issues presented by the guest speakers.

In this case, the subject matter expert, content writer, instructional designer, and director of media services all worked together to build quality materials for the new entrepreneurship course.

The previous examples outline possible outcomes for a well-functioning team. This ideal can be more difficult to achieve if there are pedagogical or personality differences among members on a team. Consider a situation in which a subject matter expert and a content writer who have been assigned to work together on a development team disagree:

> A seasoned mathematics professor is skeptical about moving toward online delivery of an introductory math course but eventually agrees to join the development team. He has been fine-tuning his teaching techniques for decades and feels that his methods for helping students manipulate formulas and equations are extremely effective. The content writer on the team has strong opinions about moving beyond formulas and equations to help students apply the math they are learning in real-world situations. Whenever the group gathers to work on the course, the majority of the meeting time is spent debating these pedagogical differences. By midterm, no clear consensus has been reached, and team members have become disillusioned with the project.

Personality differences can also impede progress on development teams. If some team members are zealous workers who are eager to build the course quickly, they may become impatient with those who lean toward a more relaxed pace. If some team members are liberal in their critical feedback, others may feel hesitant to present what they have produced. Carefully considering both the pedagogical standpoints and the personality traits of potential team members can be profitable when forming a development team.

Technology

Technology plays an indispensable role in course design and writing processes. The rapid development of new technologies raises "fundamental questions about target groups, teaching methodologies, the role and purpose of interactions and, most importantly, the question of what constitutes a quality learning experience" (White, 2003, p. 66). White emphasizes the importance of learner support systems, timely feedback, and quality interaction within a course as main goals for effective use of technology in distance learning.

Learner Support Systems.   When students enrolled in face-to-face classes have questions or need help, they have direct access to faculty members and other supportive resources. Students enrolled in online classes need similar support, which can be built into the course design. When aiming to create learner support systems, consider the following questions:

- What do faculty members do in a face-to-face environment to help students learn?
- How can that same support and scaffolding be incorporated into an online course?

Learner support may come in diverse formats and utilize a variety of technological tools. Consider the following examples.

Tutorials. While many students these days are impressively technologically savvy, faculty members cannot assume that all students will automatically know how to navigate a learning management system (LMS) effectively. Tutorials are a helpful way to provide learner support for those who need it. Within an LMS, course designers can include a module of tutorials. Students who are unfamiliar with the LMS protocols can access these short videos to learn how to use the system.

When writing tutorials, designers can make the information either course-specific or generic enough to be applicable to any course. Tutorials may answer questions such as:

- How do I update or correct the information in my profile?
- How do I make a video post?
- How do I submit a written assignment?
- How do I post to a discussion board?
- How do I join an online conference?
- How do I take a quiz?
- How do I check my grades?

While creating these training materials, writers may imagine what they would say to their students in a face-to-face setting and then include those same ideas in the tutorial. This source of "teacher talk" guides the students through technological processes and helps them to be successful in the course.

Tutoring sessions. On many campuses, students have access to tutoring services in different types of learning centers. For example, a campus-based writing center may offer one-on-one tutoring sessions in which students receive help revising and editing their writing assignments. To make this same type of learner support available to online students, additional resources at the learning centers may be required. Extra tutors could be hired to support the distance students. The online learners submit electronic copies of their written work. Tutors in the writing center make digital comments on their papers and send the feedback to the learners. Tutors could also be available for live chat to answer questions during specified learning center hours. In most cases, existing technology allows for the addition of these types of services without much cost.

Timely Feedback. In contrast to the mail-order correspondence courses of the past, technological advances have made it possible for students to receive prompt feedback on their online work. Unsurprisingly, "good teacher feedback ... promotes and improves online learning" (Vai & Sosulski, 2011, p. 131). While technology makes timely feedback possible, not all instructors are prone to utilize it to provide students with prompt and quality feedback. Faculty members are more likely to offer their students meaningful feedback if guiding parameters have been built into the course design.

Computer-generated feedback. One way to ensure that learners will receive prompt feedback is to let the computer do the scoring. Most LMSs are equipped with features that allow students to see the results of their test or quiz immediately. This type of instantaneous feedback can be especially useful for practice exercises and self-assessments. Vai and Sosulski (2011) caution, "Feedback that is generated automatically should be descriptive. Explanations accompany each answer and describe why the learner's selection was correct or incorrect" (p. 133). Faculty members who are accustomed to giving this type of descriptive commentary in class may need some in-service training on how to convert their verbal comments into online feedback that is thorough and helpful. Faculty members who have not previously created tests in the LMS may even need basic training on how to utilize those features.

Teacher feedback. When a development team designs an online course, it is not only creating course materials; it is also building the infrastructure for what teachers and students will do in the course. Therefore, if designers want teachers to have frequent communication with their students, those guidelines must be built into the course design. For example, at periodic intervals throughout the semester, students may be assigned to e-mail their teacher with a specific question or report. This would prompt the teacher to respond individually to each student's submission. The course design could also incorporate midterm conferences in which teachers meet with their students for an online chat appointment either one-on-one or in small groups. Because teachers and students may be unfamiliar with the conferencing tool used in the course, an in-depth tutorial is requisite. If departments across campus are all using the same conferencing tools, a generic tutorial can be used.

Course designers are also responsible for creating the framework that instructors will use to grade student work. This responsibility includes setting up percentages for weighted categories, ensuring that course requirements have been assigned point values, verifying that all graded assignments appear in the online grade book, and designing online rubrics within the LMS. Just as computer-generated feedback should be descriptive, teacher-generated feedback must also be clear and specific. To ensure consistency in the way online courses are graded, writers should carefully consider the type of teacher feedback that would best facilitate student learning.

Quality Interaction.   With technology today, it has become quite simple to upload large amounts of information and make that information available to students. Simply making the information available, however, does not ensure that students will engage in and absorb the content. One way to enhance an online class with a more engaging curriculum is to build opportunities for meaningful interaction into the course design. This type of interaction is important in both student-to-student and teacher-to-student exchanges.

Discussion boards. In face-to-face settings, students are often divided into pairs or small groups to discuss class content. Technological tools make it possible to facilitate similar interaction in the online setting. Consider a political science class in which students are required to read and discuss a series of weekly news articles. Within an LMS, students can be organized into groups and be assigned to make posts to discussion boards to engage in debates or other forms of group discussion. One word of caution: Even conscientious students who are diligent about posting their own assignments will not necessarily take the time to read or comment on their classmates' posts if it is not part of their grade to do so. If the goal is to facilitate interaction, it may be necessary to require students to make comments on others' work. When making comments becomes an assignment that is worth points, more students are willing to read and respond to their classmates' posts.

Audio/video uploads. With the rapid improvements in audiovisual technology, it has become quite easy to incorporate audio and video uploads into online course design. Hearing a speaker's voice and seeing that person's face help build social presence and facilitate meaningful interaction. Even in asynchronous environments, learners can post an audio or video upload and wait for an audio or video response. As with conferencing tools, administrators can support designers by allowing them to explore and choose from the various options for audio/video uploads. If a specific system is adopted campus-wide, a generic tutorial can be created and used in all online classes.

Conclusion

All in all, writing online curriculum tends to be an iterative process. When designing a new online course, writers are sure to develop some modules or activities that produce great learning success, but they will discover other course materials that need fine-tuning and revision. It is all part of the process. For this reason, members of a development team must understand the nature of the project and recognize the time commitment involved. It is also worthwhile to seek out team members with complementary skill sets and personalities to ensure productivity within the group.

Considering what teachers do in the face-to-face environment to provide enriching learning experiences can be helpful in guiding online curriculum development. Finding ways to incorporate that same type of scaffolding through teacher talk and engaging learning activities enhances the quality of online courses. Facilitating meaningful interaction is paramount so that students can actively engage in the learning process. Incorporating opportunities for teachers to provide valuable feedback will also enhance course quality. Although materials writing can be a lengthy process, for those who enjoy curriculum development it is a rewarding and exciting pursuit.

References

Allen, I. E., & Seaman, J. (2008). *Staying the course: Online education in the United States.* Needham, MA: Sloan Consortium.

Ko, S., & Rossen, S. (2010). *Teaching online: A practical guide.* New York: Routledge.

Miller, G. E., & Schiffman, S. (2006). ALN business models and the transformation of higher education. *Journal of Asynchronous Learning Networks, 10*(2), 15.

Vai, M., & Sosulski, K. (2011). *Essentials of online course design: A standards-based guide.* New York: Routledge.

White, C. (2003). *Language learning in distance education.* Cambridge, UK: Cambridge University Press.

AUBREY OLSEN BRONSON is an online instructor and curriculum developer for Brigham Young University–Hawaii.

NEW DIRECTIONS FOR HIGHER EDUCATION • DOI: 10.1002/he

6

This chapter identifies effective ways to address learner and faculty support. It introduces methods for building a successful learner support system by providing sufficient resources and proactively addressing learner motivation. It also addresses effective faculty support through institutional policies, resources, training, and course development.

Learner and Faculty Support

Sharon Guan, Daniel Stanford

Researchers have identified a strong tendency for students to withdraw from online programs due to lack of support (Jaggars & Xu, 2010). The attrition rate of online programs is 10% to 20% higher than on-ground programs (Shaik, 2012). Additionally, lack of faculty support has a direct impact on recruiting, retaining, and engaging faculty members in participating in the design and delivery of online courses.

Three essential factors were found to inhibit the success of a distance learning program at the turn of the millennium: lack of institutional support for faculty, lack of technical infrastructure, and failure to address course development (Schifter, 2000). Ten years later, a report issued by the University Leadership Council (ULC) echoed one of these findings—that motivating and adequately preparing faculty to teach online remains one of the greatest challenges for higher education institutions (University Leadership Council, 2010).

For online learners and teachers, some of the challenges are the same: both have to adjust to a learning environment that is vastly different from the traditional classroom, deal with technical issues, and adapt to written communication with fewer visual cues. They also have unique challenges due to their different roles. Yet the support needs for both groups are often intertwined: teacher support has a strong impact on learners, and vice versa. When students' problems are not addressed promptly and adequately, they quickly become those of the teacher as well (Ko & Rossen, 2010). Likewise, when a teacher's needs for pedagogical, technical, or logistical support are not addressed, students suffer the consequences. The success of online learning requires a well-developed support system for both learners and

NEW DIRECTIONS FOR HIGHER EDUCATION, no. 173, Spring 2016   © 2016 Wiley Periodicals, Inc.
Published online in Wiley Online Library (wileyonlinelibrary.com) • DOI: 10.1002/he.20180

teachers. This chapter provides an analysis of learner and faculty support needs and practical suggestions in building a system to support for both of them.

Learner Support

Learner support varies among institutions and even among programs within the same institution. When online offerings are confined to a designated unit, such as a college of continuing, professional, or distance education, learner support is generally straightforward because the unit will fund and manage support resources. Determining who will coordinate the support and how becomes a challenge when the institution seeks to engage all academic units in online learning and put a significant portion of its courses online. Administrators and support staff must recognize that a diverse collection of departments have a direct impact on the student's online learning experience—from the admissions office to financial aid to computer support (Hill, 2012).

Coordinating various support services requires a leader to identify and address online student needs through centralized university programs or at the school and college level. For example, DePaul University appointed an associate vice president in 2008 to lead the online learning mission of the university. This individual does not manage online programs, but serves as a facilitator who brings together online learning stakeholders. These include online program directors, associate deans in charge of online learning within a school or a college, and managers of online learning support units. The group is called the Online Learning Incubators and is charged with identifying and addressing faculty and learner support issues. For example, some online programs or courses require synchronous sessions where the faculty members conduct their presentations and interact with students in a virtual classroom. Since many students register for online classes expecting to complete coursework on their own schedule, the incubators raised the need to alert students of the synchronous meeting requirement in the registration system. The group then brought in the information technology (IT) units and developed the process to allow program coordinators to add this information to the registration system.

In addition to logistical support, institutions need to engage learners through instructional and emotional support. The following section identifies additional strategies that institutions can implement to optimize support and motivate students.

Optimizing Institutional Support.   Every online program needs resources for student support. For most institutions, creating a support center or position responsible for student support in each online program is unrealistic and may lead to redundancy and confusion. Through a centralized position or support unit, expertise can be solicited from various offices to develop shared resources for online learner orientation, prebuilt resources for courses, easily accessible technical support, and mechanisms for progress monitoring and intervention.

Online learner orientation. A pre-enrollment online student orientation or website is the first line of support. With questionnaires and resources, the site can help students understand the expectations of online learning and identify if it is an appropriate fit. A well-designed orientation site should also contain technology resources to help students access courses as well as tutorials on using the learning management system (Old Dominion University, n.d.-b). Some institutions offer a portal for potential students to explore various online degree options while letting individual programs provide their own orientation or information sites (DePaul University, 2014). In this case, the school or program can customize the central materials and add program-specific content such as a sample course or a space for existing students to share their online learning experiences with new or potential students (DePaul University, 2010).

Prebuilt resources for courses. Making institutional or program resources accessible through the course site enables learners to access support services whenever they encounter problems. This critical element is usually included in course review standards and reinforced through a course review process. Some course review rubrics require not only links to technical support, accessibility policies, and academic support services, but also an explanation of how these resources will help students succeed (Quality Matters, 2014). Links to these institutional resources can be added to the home page of the learning management system so that faculty members do not need to create the links in their individual courses. This also saves students the frustration of searching for support links in each course.

Easily accessible technical support. Making technical support no more than a click away is a service expected by online learners. For institutions that cannot afford a 24/7 help desk, the best and most effective approach is to develop an interactive support system that contains both video- and print-based support materials. In addition to technical support resources for the learning management system, the central support unit or a collaborative technical support group should develop a repository of support documents or tutorials for specific technologies used in the online courses. Help desk staff and course design staff should work together to clarify which tools the institution supports and which tools are being piloted without help desk support. When using unsupported tools, the instructor or the instructional designer should inform learners of the experimental nature of the project and offer alternatives if technical difficulties arise.

Mechanism for progress monitoring and intervention. Monitoring student progress through data collection is an effective way to prevent attrition. Institutions wanting to achieve high retention through effective student support should utilize the most reliable resources—their own data (ULC, 2010). When it comes to retention, the institution itself may be "the biggest single barrier to developing appropriate strategies" (Johnston & Simpson,

2006, p. 30). Identifying barriers by gathering and analyzing online learning data is a meaningful step toward enhancing academic quality and support services. In addition to gathering withdrawal rates and grades, student assessment of online learning can be administered at the end of the term (ULC, 2010). An assessment instrument can also be developed by a central support team and incorporated into the online courses as a prebuilt item. A consistent instrument allows the institution to compare programs and identify problems at the course, program, or institutional level.

Infusing Learner Motivation.   Online courses require students to take ownership of their learning through self-motivation, effective time management, and perseverance. Many students choose online learning for its convenience without recognizing the significant amount of self-discipline and persistence it requires (Ko & Rossen, 2010). To help these learners acquire the right skills and attitude for online learning, university leaders should invest in advising and faculty-driven learner support.

As tools and content become increasingly standardized, advising offers the potential for customization and individualized service (Bowen, 2012). By connecting with learners via webcam, phone, online chat, or e-mail, the adviser injects a sense of personalization into a seemingly systematic process of learning. For example, at Western Governors University, the advising role is played by "mentors" who provide academic guidance, advising, and tutoring through the programs. A mentor makes a detailed analysis of the students' background, expectations of the program, and career interests, which are gathered through a skill survey and preassessment even before they enter the program. Based on the information, the mentor conducts phone interviews with students, which lead to the creation of an Academic Action Plan for each student (Jiang, Shrader, & Parent, 2005).

Faculty members also play a critical role in improving learner motivation and should understand that motivating students is an essential part of teaching (Bowen, 2012). Because technology expands content delivery options and offers available learning resources, faculty members must learn to serve a new role—as learning coaches who devote a significant amount of time to monitoring learner progress, sending encouraging messages, rewarding learner effort, and helping students accomplish their learning goals.

This coaching methodology echoes the proactive motivational support theory, which indicates that distance learner support should be individual, interactive, and motivational (Simpson, 2008). In applying the theory, faculty can incorporate progress indicators, low-stakes assessment, checkpoints, and frequent feedback. Research has found that in motivating students, it is more effective to praise their effort than their achievement (Dweck, 1999). With the technical capacity of tracking learner activities, such as the amount of time spent on the course site, frequencies of access, number of attempts made for tests, and the quality and quantity of discussion posting, instructors can individually acknowledge the effort put in by each student or use the statistics of the most active learner as a benchmark to motivate the whole class.

Instructors can also improve learner motivation through modeling. Learners respond to teachers who are passionate about the subject and their students (Bowen, 2012). They also learn more when they recognize the information as important (Bowen, 2012; Fink, 2003; Svinicki, 1991). Faculty members can demonstrate their passion by sharing their stories about what inspired them to become an expert on the subject area or pursue a career in education. They can also point out a relevant or practical purpose for mastering a concept or completing an assignment, or identify the significance of a topic by connecting it with students' real-life experience.

Faculty Support

In addition to learner support, providing faculty members with reliable and sufficient support for online teaching requires a well-developed campus infrastructure. In many cases, successfully supporting faculty in online teaching requires making support for online learning and faculty one of the institution's strategic goals so as to ensure greater attention and support (ULC, 2010). DePaul University's VISION Twenty12 plan, for example, includes "becoming a model provider of quality distance learning" (DePaul University, n.d., p. 6). This goal led to the creation of the DePaul Online Teaching Series program, which trained 240 faculty members from 2008 to 2012. By 2012, the university's online enrollment had quadrupled, with online course offerings increasing 20% annually (Guan & Stanford, 2013).

Policies for online learning should be established well before online courses or programs are developed (ULC, 2010). These policies will direct decisions and procedures related to the use of institutional resources, training and support, legal issues (such as intellectual property rights, course ownership, and faculty compensation), and course quality.

While developing an online learning infrastructure, the institution should examine its existing faculty support mechanisms and reorganize them as needed to improve efficiency and effectiveness. At DePaul University, for example, technology training and instructional design were addressed by two distinct offices. This approach led to confusion as faculty struggled to determine which department to contact for support. By consolidating technology training and instructional design under the same office, the institution created a centralized instructional technology service unit. In this unit, instructional technology consultants are assigned or even physically embedded in various schools and programs. This structure allows faculty to receive instructional technology and course design support through a single point of contact. It emulates the most cost-effective support model suggested by ULC (2010) in terms of centralizing instructional design resources and decentralizing instructional support services.

Once the infrastructure is established, the institution can start other critical investments needed to engage faculty in online learning: training, course development, and compensation/recognition. Each of these areas requires thoughtful planning and effective implementation.

Training.   Availability of adequate training is a key factor in faculty willingness to teach online (Lee & Busch, 2005; Lloyd, Byrne, & McCoy, 2012). More than 64% of faculty members teaching online want additional opportunities for professional development (Ray, 2009). While some institutions have adopted a just-in-time approach to faculty support by providing short tutorial videos and printable software guides, this strategy fails to provide faculty with a comprehensive model of best practices in online course design and delivery.

Many award-winning faculty development programs for online learning recognize the need for faculty to experience effective online and hybrid instruction from a student perspective. To address this need, these programs often include features, time commitments, and expectations similar to those of an online course, with some requiring as much as 80 hours of coursework (DePaul University, 2009a; University of Central Florida, 2009; University of Louisiana at Lafayette, 2014). Programs may ask faculty to "participate first in the role of students, learning how to use the various features of the system, such as submitting assignments and working in study groups. They are then placed in the role of teachers, with other trainees assigned to their class" (University of Maryland University College, n.d., para. 2).

Case Study: The DePaul Online Teaching Series. The DePaul Online Teaching Series was established in 2008 to help faculty design effective online and hybrid courses. The program allows faculty to experience a model hybrid course firsthand through 18 hours of face-to-face workshops and 18 hours of online readings, videos, and discussions. The first week of the course is conducted entirely online, immersing faculty in the unique challenges of navigating a course website, identifying and meeting key deadlines, overcoming technical difficulties, participating in online discussions, and getting to know classmates without face-to-face interaction. For the remainder of the course, participants attend six face-to-face workshops and complete online assignments between meetings.

Each 3-hour workshop models effective use of in-person meeting time by focusing on activities that would be challenging to replicate online. For example, approximately half of each meeting is reserved for self-paced software practice with staff on hand to provide immediate support. This approach prevents frustration by helping faculty get unstuck quickly and ensures that participants leave the workshop more confident in their ability to complete technology-focused assignments independently. Remaining class time is used for a variety of interactive activities. Presentations typically incorporate live polls and breakout sessions for small group

7

Demand for higher education is global. As institutions extend opportunities beyond their borders, English language proficiency must be considered. This chapter focuses on considerations related to global expansion, with an emphasis on the role of distance English language courses and the distinct considerations in their development.

Global Expansion and English Language Learning

Maureen Snow Andrade

Globalization, a key reality in the 21st century, has already profoundly influenced higher education. We define globalization as the reality shaped by an increasingly integrated world economy, new information and communications technology (ICT), the emergence of an international knowledge network, the role of the English language, and other forces beyond the control of academic institutions (Altbach, Reisberg, & Rumbley, 2009, p. ii).

Although higher education institutions may not be able to control globalization forces such as the world economy, technological developments, the world knowledge network, or the position of English as an international language, as indicated in the opening quotation, they have a role in shaping these issues. Higher education is in demand worldwide due to these factors, and distance education is central. "Being able to access knowledge from any location, at any time, for any age, and in many ways, has become a requirement for individual, community, and collective well-being" (Hanna, 2013, p. 684).

Nations have widened access to encourage postsecondary education for their citizens (Corver, 2010; Higher Education Funding Council for England, 2009; Trow, 2005) to maintain and expand their competitiveness in the global knowledge economy. Individuals are seeking higher education opportunities in unprecedented numbers to experience increased employment opportunities and income, sustained employment, civic engagement, healthier lifestyles, and more satisfying family lives (Baum, Ma, & Payea, 2013). Because of English being an international language, the prevalent

NEW DIRECTIONS FOR HIGHER EDUCATION, no. 173, Spring 2016 © 2016 Wiley Periodicals, Inc.
Published online in Wiley Online Library (wileyonlinelibrary.com) • DOI: 10.1002/he.20181

language in the fields of science and technology, and the language through which much educational content is delivered, English proficiency is foundational to meeting the demand for higher education nationally and globally.

This chapter first examines areas of consideration for institutions contemplating global expansion through distance education programs. It then explores English language learning issues. The chapter concludes with implications for course design and delivery exemplified by brief case studies of institutions engaged in global distance initiatives (see Young, Chapter 8 of this volume, for an extended example).

The Case for Global Distance Learning Expansion

The demand for higher education presents a compelling case for global distance education. Worldwide enrollments increased by 53% from 2000 to 2007 (Altbach et al., 2009). The U.S. Department of Labor (2012) projects employment growth by educational qualification from 2010 to 2020 as follows: doctoral/professional—20%, master's—22%, bachelor's—17%, associate's—18%, high school—12%, less than high school—14%. By 2020, 66% of all jobs will require some form of postsecondary education (Carnevale, Smith, & Strohl, 2010). Consequently, federal and state governments and nonprofit educational organizations have set goals to increase the number of college graduates (Lee & Rawls, 2010; Lumina Foundation for Education, 2010). Outside the United States, middle-class growth and the desire to build knowledge economies in emerging nations are contributing to expanding numbers of students seeking higher education (Choudaha, Chang, & Kono, 2013). Private institutions, many of them for-profit, represent 50% to 70% of higher education enrollments in a number of nations, absorbing the need that traditional institutions cannot fill (Altbach et al., 2009).

Today's globally mobile students can access educational opportunities from a number of providers, comparing and selecting those most accessible and advantageous. Competition for these students is significant among English-speaking higher education institutions. In Australia, 24% of the undergraduate population is composed of globally mobile students, compared to 13% in the United Kingdom, 7% in Canada, and 2% in the United States (Choudaha et al., 2013). U.S. institutions "are aiming to achieve aggressive, diverse, and efficient international enrollment growth" (Choudaha et al., 2013, p. 14). This growth extends beyond serving international students on the home campus, creating a "veritable explosion in numbers of programs and institutions that are operating internationally" (Altbach et al., 2009, p. iii).

These factors—mobility, demand, competition, and expansion—suggest a vibrant market not only for face-to-face on-site delivery but for distance learning among both domestic students, of whom 33.5% are enrolled in one or more online courses (Allen & Seaman, 2013), and global students, whose overall numbers have increased by more than 50% since 2004 (Choudaha et al., 2013). The data indicate a critical need for institutions to examine their current capacities for meeting demand. For those constrained by space and resources for on-site infrastructure expansion, distance education is a solution. Such programs can address the global aim to provide higher education access (Altbach et al., 2009). Although institutional mission and governing body mandates must guide new directions and strategic planning, global educational expansion is both a need and an opportunity to improve people's lives.

Guiding Questions.   Institutions committed to globalizing their distance learning programs must consider the issues and implications. The following questions are designed to assist in this analysis. This listing assumes that the institution has an operating distance learning program with delivery mechanisms and learner and faculty support structures (e.g., see Guan and Stanford, Chapter 6 of this volume).

- *Mission.* How is global delivery supported by institutional mission or other mandates (e.g., governing board directives or policies)? Are these mandates flexible enough to accommodate new directions?
- *Infrastructure and expertise.* To what degree does the institution's infrastructure support global delivery?
  (a) Expertise in recruiting, admitting, assessing, supporting, teaching, and graduating international students.
  (b) Extensiveness of institutional contacts, networks, alumni, or infrastructure in international areas (which areas?).
- *Target countries/populations.* Which international locations make sense for the institution? How will these be determined? Who are the potential students, and what are their demographics?
- *Degree programs.* What specific degree programs and levels are in demand in the identified target areas? What is the competition from other institutions? Is there a niche market? Will new courses and programs need to be developed? If so, at what cost (see next to last bullet point)?
- *English language.* How will non-native English speakers (NNESs) be screened for appropriate academic English skills? What types of support will be available for those who need additional development? How will this support be delivered?
- *Culture.* How does the target region culture impact delivery and teaching practice, as well as learner expectations, preferences, and success (e.g., see Andrade, 2013)? What training and support are needed for faculty, staff, and students? What are the cultural expectations for communication and social presence, and how can community building be supported among the learners, faculty, and institution (e.g., see Gunawardena, 2013).
- *Technology.* What global location-specific constraints or opportunities exist regarding technology?

(a) Currency and availability of technology.
(b) Learner familiarity with technology.
(c) Extent, quality, and reliability of on-site technology infrastructure and providers.

- *Learner support.* What types of learner support are needed (e.g., technology, library access, advisement, counseling, learning assistance centers, tutoring, mentoring)? How are these similar to or different from existing forms of support?

- *Costs.* What costs and resources are involved? Are economies of scale expected? What revenues are anticipated? What is the return on investment? What factors affect cost, and how will costs be calculated (e.g., see Jung & Lee, 2013)? How does delivery to developing or developed nations affect this return?

- *Quality.* What are the quality concerns, and how will these be addressed? What accreditation issues exist? How will these be resolved? What changes are needed in institutional policy?

This listing provides a foundation for examining issues surrounding global distance learning. Although some of these factors apply to all distance learning, they must be viewed through an international lens to determine the feasibility of global expansion. Institutions should complete a thorough review of their existing distance education operations to ensure that they are responsive to the needs of identified target-area countries and students.

A Primer on English Language Learning

"International rankings favour universities that use English as the main language of instruction and research" (Altbach et al., 2009, p. iii). English-medium institutions are sought after by globally mobile students, creating global competition to attract them. Academic English proficiency is a necessary prerequisite for students to succeed in these contexts, and institutions must provide the means for this to occur. This section provides an overview of key issues related to English language learning: language acquisition, proficiency testing, and linguistic challenges. These topics are discussed both generally and in distance education contexts.

Language Acquisition.   English language learning through distance or online delivery has unique requirements, notably the need for interaction and communicative practice. Although teacher-to-learner and learner-to-learner interaction is an asset to all distance courses for community building and content mastery, interactive learning components and a language-rich environment are critical to language acquisition.

For language acquisition to occur, three elements must be present: (1) comprehensible input in the form of reading and listening at the learner's current level of proficiency (Krashen, 1985); (2) output through speaking and writing for purposes of testing linguistic rules and experiencing language usage in different social contexts (Swain, 1995); and (3) meaning negotiation through target language communication, which results in direct or indirect feedback about comprehensibility and leads to the adjustment of linguistic output (Long, 1996). The opportunities for input, output, and meaning testing are limited in non-English speaking and distance or online learning environments.

Another consideration for language learning is the difference between social and academic English. The former, referred to as basic interpersonal communication skills (BICS), consists of everyday, conversational language, whereas the latter, known as cognitive academic language proficiency (CALP), is much more demanding and complex (Cummins, 2008). It entails the ability to manage complex language in terms of register, text genres, and vocabulary while focused on abstract and often unfamiliar concepts. BICS can be acquired with a target language exposure of approximately 2 years, whereas CALP requires 5 or more years. Learners who have achieved BICS cannot be assumed to be fluent in CALP. Consider the difference in language tasks in the two realms. A task requiring BICS might consist of asking directions, conversing about one's family or plans for the weekend, or managing a daily transaction (e.g., shopping, banking, household repairs). A typical CALP task involves the ability to synthesize and critically evaluate arguments in a specialized academic area using grammatically accurate spoken and written language and formal register in sentence structure and vocabulary.

Plentiful opportunities for input and output must be included in the course design and supported by appropriate technology. The amount of time required to acquire academic English is applicable in both face-to-face and distance contexts; however, considering that distance learners are most likely living in non-English-speaking environments, the need for communicative practice is even greater in order to compensate. Institutions must carefully consider these issues and related opportunities.

Proficiency Testing.   "It has been decided that if they [non-native English speakers] meet our admissions criteria, they have demonstrated adequate English understanding and as such no further monitoring is performed" (Andrade, Evans, & Hartshorn, 2014, p. 214). Although one might argue that standardized proficiency tests and admission standards address the issue of English language proficiency and no further support is needed, as indicated in this quotation, many institutions, including those hosting the most NNESs in the United States, recognize that screening on this basis is problematic and often fails to provide an accurate assessment of linguistic skill (Andrade et al., 2014).

Scores on standardized tests represent a range of proficiency. Therefore, a student's true score may be higher or lower than the reported score. This argues against the use of rigid admission cutoff scores. Similarly, standardized English proficiency tests may measure passive knowledge of English rather than the ability to use the language. Improvement in this area has occurred, however. The Test of English as a Foreign Language (TOEFL) now reflects academic tasks that learners will encounter. Students are asked to respond to speaking and writing tasks using information from reading passages and short lectures, which is reflective of a higher education learning environment. Even so, additional measures administered after admission, with the involvement of English as a second language (ESL) professionals, is strongly recommended to triangulate the data from a single test and to account for the standard errors of measure.

In terms of current higher education practice, institutions predominantly use standardized tests, specifically the TOEFL (Andrade et al., 2014). About one third use two methods of testing, and half require post-admissions testing, with writing measures being twice as common as speaking. These practices address the issue of "not getting a true assessment of … students' academic language skills" (Andrade et al., 2014, p. 216), and students having impressive test scores, but "very low English abilities" (p. 216). Although additional testing may be unpopular with students, the following quotation illustrates a responsible approach to this issue: "We believe a disappointed student is better than a failing student" (p. 216).

Linguistic Challenges.   Learners' English proficiency contributes to the challenges they face in academic contexts. Areas of concern include academic, social, and cultural (Andrade, 2006; Andrade & Evans, 2007; Andrade et al., 2014; Holta, 2013), which overlap and are affected by linguistic skill.

Academic issues include teaching and learning styles; unfamiliarity with classroom discourse in terms of questioning and interaction patterns; rapidity of speech, idiomatic expressions, and unfamiliar allusions; the need for processing time prior to response; expectations for critical thinking, synthesis of knowledge, and original thought; amount of required reading coupled with slower reading speeds and limited vocabulary knowledge; and peer collaboration. These behaviors and practices may be different from those in the learners' educational systems. Socially, international NNESs may have difficulty forming friendships and may keep to themselves, resulting in feelings of isolation and homesickness. They may lack confidence in their English skills, which compounds both academic and social interaction. Differing views of friendship, values, and cultural practices affect life within and outside the classroom.

How do these factors impact online learning for NNESs? They may be mitigated if learners are in their own countries where adjustment to daily cultural differences is not a factor. Issues related to academic expectations such as teaching and learning styles and course requirements are pertinent, however, as are the English skills needed to navigate online courses. The latter may require greater independence than students are accustomed to, as well as the ability to control the factors that affect their learning—that is, self-regulated learning (SRL) (Dembo, Junge, & Lynch, 2006).

New Directions for Higher Education • DOI: 10.1002/he

Implications for Design and Delivery

Institutions designing and delivering online courses for NNESs in their home countries must consider issues of learner support. This section discusses stand-alone and integrated English language support and the need for self-regulation. These components are illustrated with case studies.

English Language Support. One of the most direct ways to support English language proficiency development is to provide required distance English language courses prior to enrollment in degree programs. Course design must center on needed language acquisition components. This entails ensuring that the course equally represents the four strands of a well-balanced language course: meaning-focused input, meaning-focused output, language-focused instruction, and fluency development (Nation, 2001). In other words, courses must provide opportunities for learners to comprehend input through reading and speaking; communicate meaning through speaking and writing; receive formal instruction in the rules, systems, and structure of the language; and develop fluency in listening, reading, writing, and speaking using language already acquired.

Another approach to supporting English language development is to integrate it into discipline-based courses (e.g., see Andrade, Evans, & Hartshorn, 2015; Arkoudis, Baik, & Richardson, 2012). This might include providing learners with vocabulary study for comprehension of readings and lectures, organization and grammar instruction specific to writing assignments, reading text organization help, and strategies for lecture comprehension. As opposed to add-on models, this approach has greater direct relevance to learners.

Self-Regulated Learning. Distance learners need to be self-regulated and assume responsibility for factors that affect their success. Self-regulated learning (SRL) theory, consisting of six dimensions, provides a useful framework for course design and instructor facilitation of the learning process. The six areas—motive (purposes for learning and goals), methods (strategies for deeper levels of processing and information retention), time (priorities, scheduling, and time management), physical environment (awareness and elimination of distractors), social environment (when and from whom to seek help), and performance (self-evaluation, monitoring, and adjusting goals and strategies) (Dembo et al., 2006; Zimmerman, 1994)—can be incorporated into online courses.

Autonomy, which can be conceptualized on a spectrum encompassing limited choice on one end and self-direction on the other, is a related concept, and interacts with structure and dialogue to diminish the transactional distance between the learner and the instructor (Moore, 2013). Structure consists of established content and organizational elements such as teaching units, presentations, exercises, activities, and deadlines. When these offer limited learner choice or decision making, autonomy is low. Dialogue involves learner–instructor interaction through discussion forums, announcements, e-mail exchanges, technology-mediated live interactive tutoring sessions or office hours, and assignment feedback. When dialogue is extensive, learner autonomy is low, as learners are dependent on teacher direction. Autonomy does not imply complete independence or a lack of support but rather a state of interdependence between teacher and learner (Little, 1995), or what some have referred to as collaborative control (White, 2003).

For English language learners accustomed to teacher-centered models or cultural educational practices that do not involve learner responsibility, choice, or decision making, transactional distance can be problematic. Thus, course design that includes learning tools based on theoretical principles is advantageous.

Case Studies.   Elements of English language and self-regulated learning support are evident in two global online distance education programs, one at Brigham Young University Hawaii and the other at Brigham Young University Idaho (see Young, Chapter 8 in this volume for a description of the latter). Both are designed to extend affordable access to learners in developing countries, and provide stand-alone English language courses that are prerequisites to further study.

In terms of language acquisition, specifically the four strands, the courses provide input in the form of readings, written and verbal instruction, teacher and student dialogue, narrated and scripted PowerPoint presentations, and scripted videos; output occurs through writing assignments, live interactive tutoring and conferencing, learner discussion forums, collaborative group projects, and video postings. Formal and direct instruction in grammar, vocabulary, discourse patterns, and reading skills related to chapter themes and assignments are included. Fluency development occurs with a culminating assignment for each unit based on the sequenced instruction, models, and practice activities.

The institutions have also developed support beyond English language instruction using models with similar purposes but different theoretical underpinnings. Both address the need for learners to possess a degree of autonomy or responsibility for factors that affect their learning. The models support the principle of collaborative control (White, 2003) to encourage learners to work together on tasks and activities. The instructor facilitates rather than directs. For example, rather than marking or correcting student errors on a writing assignment, the instructor might provide examples of incorrect and correct structures and ask learners to find and revise similar instances in their own writing.

Online courses from Brigham Young University Hawaii incorporate the six SRL dimensions explained previously (Andrade, 2014). These serve as the backbone for the course design. Learners are introduced to and practice strategies in each of the areas, set and reflect on goals, and monitor their performance. Thus, they acquire language skills while increasing their capacity for autonomy. The Brigham Young University Idaho model consists

NEW DIRECTIONS FOR HIGHER EDUCATION • DOI: 10.1002/he

of a three-step process: preparing individually for course assignments, having students teach each other, and pondering and reflecting. Learners engage with their peers, share insights and questions, and act as both learners and teachers. They are assessed on what they are taught, and reflect on their progress. Both models demonstrate that online learning is not learning on one's own, but involves collaborating with others. Both address cultural adjustment needs by focusing on learner-centered rather than teacher-centered pedagogy.

Conclusion

This chapter has introduced issues related to global expansion of distance learning with an emphasis on English language acquisition. Institutions must conduct a careful needs analysis, consider the target learner's support requirements, and develop distance programs accordingly. Opportunity and demand for such programs are evident. Distance education "is inclusive, reaching individuals previously marginalized to change lives and improve communities and economies" (Andrade, 2013, p. 67). Institutions must determine if this opportunity is appropriate to their current mission or to an expanded vision, and whether it is advisable to fulfill the role of higher education, benefit the global community, and expand access and opportunity.

References

Allen, I. E., & Seaman, J. (2013). *Grade change: Tracking online education in the United States*. Babson Park, MA: Babson Survey Research Group and Quahog Research Group. Retrieved from http://sloanconsortium.org/publications/survey/grade-change-2013

Altbach, P. G., Reisberg, L., & Rumbley, L. E. (2009). *Trends in global higher education: Tracking an academic revolution*. Paris: UNESCO.

Andrade, M. S. (2006). International students in English-speaking universities: Adjustment factors. *Journal of Research in International Education, 5*(2), 131–154.

Andrade, M. S. (2013). Global learning by distance: Principles and practicalities for learner support. *International Journal of Online Pedagogy and Course Design, 3*(1), 66–81.

Andrade, M. S. (2014, April). *International eLearning: Models for success*. Proceedings of the 6th International Conference on Computer Supported Education, Barcelona, Spain (pp. 7–14).

Andrade, M., & Evans, N. (2007). University instructors' views of ESL students: Implications for training. In G. Poedjosoedarmo (Ed.), *Teacher education in language teaching, anthology series 48* (pp. 224–249). Singapore: SEAMEO Regional Language Centre.

Andrade, M. S., Evans, N., & Hartshorn, J. (2014). ESL students in higher education: Institutional approaches to a population at-risk. *Journal of Student Affairs Research and Practice, 51*(2), 207–221.

Andrade, M. S., Evans, N., & Hartshorn, J. (2015). Perceptions and realities of ESL students in higher education: An overview of institutional practices. In N. Evans, N. Anderson, & W. Eggington (Eds.), *ESL readers and writers in higher education: Understanding challenges, providing support* (pp. 18–35). New York: Routledge.

Arkoudis, S., Baik, C., & Richardson, S. (2012). *English language standards in higher education: From entry to exit*. Camberwell, Australia: Australian Council for Educational Research.

Baum, S., Ma, J., & Payea, K. (2013). *Education pays 2013: The benefits of higher education for individuals and society*. New York: College Board. Retrieved from http://trends.collegeboard.org/sites/default/files/education-pays-2013-full-report.pdf

Carnevale, A. P., Smith, N., & Strohl, J. (2010, June). *Help wanted: Projections of jobs and education requirements through 2018*. Washington, DC: Georgetown University Center on Education and the Workforce. Retrieved from http://cew.georgetown.edu/jobs2018/

Choudaha, R., Chang, L., & Kono, Y. (2013, March). International student mobility trends 2013: Towards responsive recruitment strategies. *World Education News & Review, 26*(2). Retrieved from http://www.wes.org/ewenr/13mar/feature.htm

Corver, M. (2010). *Trends in young participation in higher education: Core results for England*. Bristol, UK: Higher Education Funding Council for England. Retrieved from http://www.hefce.ac.uk/pubs/hefce/2010/10_03/

Cummins, J. (2008). BICS and CALP: Empirical and theoretical status of the distinction. In B. Street & N. H. Hornberger (Eds.), *Encyclopedia of language and education: Vol. 2. Literacy* (2nd ed., pp. 71–83). New York: Springer-Verlag.

Dembo, M. H., Junge, L. G., & Lynch, R. (2006). Becoming a self-regulated learner: Implications for web-based education. In H. F. O'Neil & R. S. Perez (Eds.), *Web-based learning: Theory, research, and practice* (pp. 185–202). Mahwah, NJ: Lawrence Erlbaum Associates.

Gunawardena, C. N. (2013). Culture and online distance language learning. In M. G. Moore (Ed.), *Handbook of distance education* (3rd ed., pp. 185–200). New York: Routledge.

Hanna, D. E. (2013). Emerging organizational models in higher education. In M. G. Moore (Ed.), *Handbook of distance education* (3rd ed., pp. 684–694). New York: Routledge.

Higher Education Funding Council for England. (2009). *Strategic plan 2006–11*. Bristol, UK: Author. Retrieved from http://www.hefce.ac.uk/pubs /hefce /2009/09_21/

Holta, J. (2013). Intercultural adjustment and friendship dialectics in international students: A qualitative study. *International Journal of Intercultural Relations, 37*(5), 550–567.

Jung, I., & Lee, S. (2013). Cost-effectiveness of online education. In M. G. Moore (Ed.), *Handbook of distance education* (3rd ed., pp. 521–532). New York: Routledge.

Krashen, S. (1985). *The input hypothesis: Issues and implications*. London, UK: Longman.

Lee, J. M., & Rawls, A. (2010). *The college completion agenda, 2010 progress report*. National College Board Advocacy and Policy Center. Retrieved from http://completionagenda.collegeboard.org/sites/default/files/reports_pdf/Progress_Report_2010.pdf

Little, D. (1995). Learning as dialogue: The dependence of learner autonomy on teacher autonomy. *System, 23*(2), 175–181.

Long, M. (1996). The role of the linguistic environment in second language acquisition. In W. Ritchie & T. Bhatia (Eds.), *Handbook of second language acquisition* (pp. 413–468). San Diego, CA: Academic Press.

Lumina Foundation for Education. (2010, September). *A stronger nation through higher education*. Retrieved from http://www.luminafoundation.org/states_landing/a_stronger_nation_through_education/

Moore, M. G. (2013). The theory of transactional distance. In M. G. Moore (Ed.), *Handbook of distance education* (3rd ed., pp. 66–85). New York: Routledge.

Nation, I. S. P. (2001). *Learning vocabulary in another language*. Cambridge University Press.

Swain, M. (1995). Three functions of output in second language learning. In G. Cook & B. Seidlhofer (Eds.), *For H. G. Widdowson: Principles and practice in the study of language* (pp. 125–144). Oxford, UK: Oxford University Press.

Trow, M. A. (2005). *Reflections on the transition from elite to mass to universal access: Forms and phases of higher education in modern societies since WWII.* Berkeley, CA: Institute of Governmental Studies, UC Berkeley. Retrieved from http://escholarship .org/uc/item/96p3s213

U.S. Department of Labor. (2012). *Occupational outlook handbook.* Retrieved from http://www.bls.gov/ooh/About/Projections-Overview.htm#educationandtraining

White, C. (2003). *Language learning in distance education.* Cambridge: Cambridge University Press.

Zimmerman, B. J. (1994). Dimensions of academic self-regulation: A conceptual framework for education. In D. H. Schunk, & B. J. Zimmerman (Eds.), *Self-regulation of learning and performance* (pp. 3–21). Hillsdale, NJ: Lawrence Erlbaum.

MAUREEN SNOW ANDRADE is associate vice president of Academic Affairs for Academic Programs at Utah Valley University. Her responsibilities include distance learning, faculty development, assessment, curriculum development, degree completion, general education, and graduate studies.

8

This chapter provides a case study of innovation using eLearning in higher education. The case study shows how one university made system-wide organizational and procedural changes to create low-cost, open-access distance learning opportunities on a global level in response to student needs and opportunities.

Innovation and Global eLearning: A Case Study at Brigham Young University–Idaho

Alan L. Young

Through a series of innovations, Brigham Young University–Idaho (BYU-Idaho) has become a global, student-centered university. The innovations have been built on foundational principles in place from the university's beginnings as a local, rural, student-centered college. The first principal of the school, Jacob Spori, saw the impact of the university in the lives of the students, and perhaps was envisioning a future day when he said, "The seeds we're planting today will grow and become mighty oaks and their branches will run all over the earth" (Crowder, 1997, p. 3).

BYU-Idaho is a religious institution sponsored by the Church of Jesus Christ of Latter-Day Saints. Originally, the school was a 2-year junior college, Ricks College, serving a few thousand students a year. These students primarily came from the areas immediately surrounding the school. Over time, the 2-year college began to serve students from around the United States and from various foreign countries who would travel to the small Idaho home of the college for a religious-based, student-centered higher education experience. During this period, enrollments grew to near 10,000. In 2000, the school became a 4-year baccalaureate-granting institution. Through these periods, university leaders saw a future where the institution would find a way to extend the opportunities of higher education beyond the small campus.

With an eye to the future, in 1971, Ricks College President Henry B. Eyring anticipated a day when the school would serve students from many circumstances and cultures, and even those who would not come to the campus in Idaho (Eyring, 1971). In 1998, prior to guiding the transition from 2-year Ricks College to 4-year BYU-Idaho, President David A. Bednar

NEW DIRECTIONS FOR HIGHER EDUCATION, no. 173, Spring 2016 © 2016 Wiley Periodicals, Inc.
Published online in Wiley Online Library (wileyonlinelibrary.com) • DOI: 10.1002/he.20182

87

noted that the university would one day "bless the lives of tens of thousands of young Latter-day Saints throughout the world. We must learn to assist and bless institute students and other LDS youth in Rhode Island and Rome while effectively serving our students on campus in Rexburg" (Bednar, 1998, "More Students Must Be Blessed" section, para. 1).

Finally, in 2005, the current university president, Kim B. Clark, described a new phase of the university: "We will find new ways to use information technology to reach more students and to deepen the learning experience of those we touch. In a day not far from now, we will be able to break down the barriers of time and space and ... create outstanding, interactive educational experiences. In these experiences students will teach one another in new and powerful ways" (Clark, 2005).

University-Wide Imperatives for Access, Cost, and Quality

President Clark led the university in taking specific steps toward the future of growth and development that he, and past presidents, had envisioned. Clark focused the attention of the university around three imperatives. First, serve more students. Second, reduce the relative cost of education for the students. Third, substantially raise the quality of the student experience (Clark, 2005). Across the university, faculty and staff began to refine their existing processes to better accomplish these imperatives.

At the same time, a specific new initiative was launched in the university in the form of eLearning, or online learning as it was called at the university. This initiative was designed to address each of these imperatives at the same time in an innovative way. The projection was that some form of online learning could be a catalyst to enable the university to make large strides in all three imperatives at once. The hope was that the university could serve more students by going to them in their homes, rather than bringing to rural Idaho all of the students who desired the religious-based higher educational experience the school offered. It was anticipated that the cost of the educational experience could go down with the prospect of not adding additional bricks-and-mortar facilities, through the economies of scale afforded by serving more students, and through efficiencies in the course delivery. The quality of the learning experience was anticipated as the most important factor, and was projected to see increases through a focused course design process, close alignment with the university-wide learning model, a team approach to course design and delivery, and systematic, ongoing evaluation and course improvement efforts (Young, Galbraith, & Adams, 2012).

Disruptive Innovation

An early leader of the online learning initiative was Clark Gilbert, a protégé of Clayton Christensen and his work on disruptive innovation

NEW DIRECTIONS FOR HIGHER EDUCATION • DOI: 10.1002/he

(Christensen, 1997). Gilbert brought a rich background of applying disruptive innovation in various settings, in particular the newspaper industry and its transition from the traditional print publication to digital distribution. Gilbert saw how a disruptive innovation could be established within the university to make major progress toward increased access, reduced cost, and improved quality. Online learning became the environment, and the catalyst, for the disruptive innovation.

BYU-Idaho had experimented with online courses since 2000. In 2008, a separate entity was established at the university to focus exclusively on online learning. This followed the disruptive innovation model of establishing a new entity separate and distinct from the parent organization (Christensen, 1997). The organization would function separately and independently within the university, but would include strategic connection points to key components of the parent BYU-Idaho organization. The new online learning organization was tasked with establishing a model for creating high-quality online courses that could scale to thousands of students in a cost-effective way.

Prior to this, BYU-Idaho had worked within a traditional university model to dabble in online learning approaches. Faculty interested in this medium would utilize existing course materials or build new course materials and teach an online section much like they would a face-to-face section. Interest ebbed and flowed, and the quality of the courses ranged from very poor to very good, with a wide variety of results. This approach did not allow any additional students to be served, and the cost of providing the experience remained essentially the same as offering face-to-face courses.

The disruptive innovation through online learning had three core characteristics: standardized course development, integrated curriculum, and remote online instructors (J. Gilbert, 2007).

Standardized Course Development.   A course development team was organized that included instructional designers and developers, project managers, and reviewers (copy-editing, copyright, Americans With Disabilities Act requirements, etc.). Course standards for all online course delivery were developed and tested. A systematic process for designing, producing, and maintaining volumes of online courses was created. The process created an environment where project managers and instructional designers would partner with full-time faculty to create courses that would be engaging and effective for students, and also be able to scale to thousands of additional students. For example, the core curriculum was the same for each online course. Also, courses were designed around strategies where students could be actively engaged in activities in their own location or via online communication tools, but were intentionally kept low bandwidth to facilitate growth into diverse areas of the world. The activities the students participated in and accomplished became the core of the course design, with readings as a content foundation for the learning activities. Graphics, video, and animations were used sparingly, but carefully and intentionally, to provide strategically placed motivational sparks, illustrations, or other visual enhancements.

Integrated Curriculum.   The standardized online curriculum was integrated with the curriculum used on campus. The outcomes were the same. Core assessments to demonstrate student achievement of the outcomes were exactly the same or similar enough to be comparable. Content was similar enough to be familiar and aligned, though leaving enough flexibility to take advantage of the benefits of the online medium. The integrated curriculum strategy allowed the university to use existing programs and accreditation, and simply extend those programs through online learning methods. All of the curriculum was based in the university-wide learning model. The learning model, established in 2007, was a shared language for thinking about and improving the learning experience across the university. It was based on principles of sound learning and teaching involving active student participation in the learning experience, and processes of regular preparation, teaching others, and proving one's own learning. For the disruptive online learning innovation, the common outcomes became the key touch point with the parent organization, along with department approval of courses and full-time faculty involvement in the course creation and maintenance process.

Remote Online Instructors.   The instructors of the online courses would be distributed across the country, and potentially around the world. A typical instructor would be employed in the instructor's profession and teach one section of a course on the side. Potential instructors were evaluated and trained in the practices of teaching online and in a course design grounded in the university's learning model. Existing instructors had ongoing development to refine their skills. Instructors were organized into teaching groups to form a community bond and to assist each other. With a standardized, though adaptable, curriculum, the role of the instructor was that of an expert in the discipline, an effective and compassionate course facilitator, and, most important, one who could lift and inspire students. In this element of the disruptive innovation, department chair approval of all online instructor hires became the key connection point with the parent organization.

This disruptive approach to online learning yielded almost immediate results. The quality of the student experience was very good, though it came to that point through a rapid learning process in the first few semesters. Each course was analyzed, revised, and adjusted, and quality improved quickly. All course development and delivery, along with the corresponding infrastructure, were created with scalability in mind. And, at least on paper in various financial projections, the model seemed to support a substantially more cost-effective approach compared to the on-campus experience.

but the academic department described a recommended path through the degree. This reduced student options, but focused attention on the most common options and therefore improved efficiency, reducing the number of online courses to build, maintain, and deliver.

This streamlined degree approach also highlighted incremental success points for students. The bachelor's degree was a very long-range goal for most online degree students. That process was broken up into smaller steps, with practical and useful achievements along the way. With good planning, the student's first 15 credits could produce an official certificate, a useful credential to improve job opportunities. Those 15 credits would apply directly to an applied associate's degree, the next step of achievement. This would become a second practical credential to utilize as the student moved ahead with life, while also pursuing the next phase of education. An additional certificate could be earned with the classes taken toward a bachelor's degree. Finally, all the credits, having been put to good use along the way, are applied toward a bachelor's degree.

One of the initial goals was to serve more students. In 2011, just over 4,000 students were enrolled in online courses. By 2013, that number was approaching 10,000. Enrollment patterns in 2014 suggested there would be more than 16,000 students. In 2011, half of the students in online classes were on-campus students enrolled in online classes. By the end of 2013, only 30% were on-campus, with the rest taking their classes through BYU-Idaho online. This outreach goes to students throughout the United States, and in countries throughout North and South America, Africa, and Europe.

An Integrated Future

The disruptive innovation at BYU-Idaho created an environment that allowed for rapid changes in a new course delivery mode that generated a high-quality experience, increased student access, and cost efficiencies. With the maturation of the innovations, it became time to create closer integrations of functions across the university. However, this would not be integration to the previous methods of doing the business of the university. The path had been forged, and the BYU-Idaho was serving a very different type of student body. Each constituent part of the university would have to grasp the implications of working with the new student body, draw from lessons learned in the innovation phase, and continually adapt and adjust their processes to accomplish the university's mission and established growth pattern.

BYU-Idaho is one example of a disruptive innovation applied in higher education. The end result of these innovations has allowed the university to create low-cost, open-access, distance learning opportunities for students on a global level. While a few aspects of the innovation and change are unique to BYU-Idaho's environment, most of the principles described could be effectively applied in any setting. In summary, some of those key principles are:

- Establish a disruptive, or separate, environment as a catalyst for change.
- Define the target student population.
- Focus on core goals, and create an evaluation plan to measure progress.
- Establish common quality criteria.
- Decouple teaching practices (curriculum development, course facilitation, feedback, management) and develop specializations.
- Utilize existing technologies to overcome traditional barriers.
- Start small and run a lot of tests and pilots.

The importance of higher education in society is increasing. Educational institutions can implement changes such as those illustrated here to better satisfy the need at an increasing level of quality.

References

Bednar, D. A. (1998, February 27). *Inaugural response.* Retrieved from http://www2 .byui.edu/Presentations/Transcripts/Inauguration/1998_02_27_Bednar.html

Christensen, C. M. (1997). *The innovator's dilemma: When new technologies cause great firms to fail.* Boston, MA: Harvard Business Review Press.

Clark, K. B. (2005, October 11). *Inaugural response.* Retrieved from http://www.byui.edu /Presentations/Transcripts/MiscellaneousAddresses/2005_10_11_Clark.htm

Crowder, D. L. (1997). *The spirit of Ricks: A history of Ricks College.* Rexburg, ID: Ricks College Press.

Eyring, H. B. (1971, December 10). *Inaugural response.* Video retrieved from https://co ntent.byui.edu/items/23476c00-6c16-44da-af7b-f931688ca0b2/1/?.vi=kalturaViewer &attachment.uuid=e7e4a5fd-4dfd-46dc-a6bb-24669032a417

Eyring, H. J. (2007). A vision of online learning. *Perspective Magazine, 7*(1), 56–64. Retrieved from http://www.byui.edu/Documents/instructional_development /Perspective/V7n1PDF/v7n1_eyring.pdf

Gilbert, J. (2007). Online learning report. *Perspective Magazine, 7*(1), 65–71. Retrieved from http://www.byui.edu/Documents/instructional_development/Perspective/V7n1P DF/v7n1_gilbert.pdf

Griffith, J. D., & Howard, D. (2011). The Pathway program. *Perspective Magazine, 11*(2). Retrieved from http://www.byui.edu/Documents/instructional_development /Perspective/Fall%202011/J.D%20Griffith.pdf

Young, A. L., Galbraith, J., & Adams, S. (2012). BYU-Idaho's evolving approach to online course quality. *Perspective Magazine* (Fall), 24–28. Retrieved from http://www.byui .edu/Documents/instructional_development/Perspective/Fall%202012/6%20BYU-Ida ho's%20Evolving%20Approach.pdf

ALAN L. YOUNG *is the online learning managing director at Brigham Young University–Idaho.*

9

This chapter describes technological disruptions in higher education that pose challenges and offer opportunities to college and university students, faculty, and administrators. It provides examples of innovative responses being explored by 2-year and 4-year higher education institutions.

On the Cutting Edge: Movements and Institutional Examples of Technological Disruption

Marjorie Roth Leon, Todd Alan Price

Legend tells of Yameel, famed African runner. Swift and reliable, Yameel could deliver a message to anybody anywhere. One day an elder came upon Yameel standing stock-still in the middle of the road. "Why have you stopped?" queried the elder. "You have urgent messages to deliver!" Yameel replied: "I have been running so fast that I have left my soul behind. I am waiting for it to catch up to me" (Schwartz & Hass, 2001, p. 109).

Like Yameel, technological innovation has been running so fast that society—the *soul* of civilization—has struggled to keep pace. The term *disruptive technology* describes this rapid innovation. It refers to technological advances that offer such superior efficiency and effectiveness that they render older products and processes obsolete (Bower & Christensen, 1995). An example is Gutenberg's invention of movable type, which enabled parishioners to read the King James Bible asynchronously and interpret passages on their own—an early form of student-centered learning. Recently, e-mail has eliminated the wait time and expense associated with snail mail: In a mere 40 years, it has displaced how civilization has handled written communication for the past 4,000 years.

Blin and Munro (2008) argue that "education seems to be 'the last frontier' for technological disruption" (cited in Honeycutt & Glova, 2014, p. 2). Honeycutt and Glova (2014) speculate that higher education has embraced technological disruption slowly because of a conservative stance toward change, the desire for data supporting the adoption of digitized learning, perceived lack of support for design and delivery of quality digitized

New Directions for Higher Education, no. 173, Spring 2016 © 2016 Wiley Periodicals, Inc.
Published online in Wiley Online Library (wileyonlinelibrary.com) • DOI: 10.1002/he.20183

learning, and a belief that digitized instruction creates faculty–student barriers. To examine the impact of disruptive technology on higher education, we pose two questions: (1) How does technological disruption impact students, faculty members, and administrators at institutions of higher education? (2) How are faculty members and administrators responding deliberatively to the digitization of higher education? We answer these questions by examining the literature related to technological innovations; conducting interviews with higher education administrators, instructional design team members, and directors of online education initiatives; and collecting anecdotal information volunteered by administrators and faculty members at our own university. These insights are intended to assist higher education professionals actively seeking ways to effectively and deliberatively leverage the benefits that technological disruption can provide.

Technological Disruption in Higher Education: A Brief History

Elizabeth Harrison, founder of the National College of Education, drove a horse and buggy to deliver the message that kindergarten was important—a low-tech form of distance education. The U.S. postal service played a role in early distance education that eerily foreshadowed modern-day massive open online courses (MOOCs):

> The spread of a powerful new communication network—the modern postal system—had made it possible for universities to distribute their lessons beyond the bounds of their campuses. ... Sensing a historic opportunity to reach new students and garner new revenues, schools rushed to set up correspondence divisions. By the 1920s, postal courses had become a full-blown mania. Four times as many people were taking them as were enrolled in all the nation's colleges and universities combined (Carr, 2012, p. 1).

Using distinctly modern language, correspondence courses promised that students would "receive individual personal attention" delivered "according to any personal schedule and in any place where postal service is available," offering students "an intimate 'tutorial relationship' that takes into account individual differences in learning" (Carr, 2012, p. 1).

Today's distance education technologies can deliver information in nanoseconds to massive audiences. Despite changes in modalities of instructional content delivery, expanding data and knowledge creation, and vast advances in electronic communication and social media, the goal of distance education remains to provide individualized instruction *anytime, anywhere.*

Technological Disruptions: Impact on Students

In our interview, Dean S. said that "technology itself isn't the big disrupter. The [economic] recession has brought about a perfect storm—one in which higher education has reached the boundaries of affordability for many" with "the value and cost of a higher education degree in the United States being questioned by students, employers, and the federal government." Portable, low-cost electronic devices that allow education to be delivered asynchronously at reduced cost and at a distance enable an increased number of people to participate in higher education. Following are examples illustrating deliberative responses that benefit students.

Competency-Based Online Programs.   Dean S.'s large state university is experimenting with fully online competency-based programs in which the pairing of distance learning with competency-based education constitutes the technological disruption. An instructional support team assigns academic success coaches with master's degrees and some disciplinary knowledge to all entry-level students. Coaches use a university learning management system (LMS)-supported dashboard to monitor a caseload of 100 students weekly and scaffold student access to successive levels of team resources as needed, including tutors, life coaches, and faculty members. Students enrolled in this program are encouraged to learn through instructional strategies and informational resources they find effective. Prior knowledge can be applied to pass a course by examination, and some students have waived a full-semester course this way. Program content is mapped and broken down into individual competencies, a best-practice process in distance education (Quality Matters, 2014; Vai & Sosulski, 2011).

An instructional design team at a community college addresses limited student study time by offering online courses via *lecture capture*, in which class lectures and content displayed on faculty members' computer screens are electronically recorded. Students retrieve the online televised lesson for viewing at any time through a web link. This asynchronous learning opportunity allows students to maintain a balance among competing school, work, and family demands and to repeat the electronic lesson as needed for mastery.

Open Source Materials.   Open source materials are free or low-cost courseware. In 2012, Rice University and its open source materials publisher, OpenStax, pioneered a project funded by grants from four major corporations. OpenStax advertises that it "offers students free textbooks that meet scope and sequence requirements for most courses. ... Free online and low-cost in print, OpenStax College books are built for today's student budgets" (Rice University, 2014, p. 1). Numerous American community colleges, private universities, and state universities, as well as international universities, use OpenStax course materials.

In May 2012, the University of Minnesota established an online catalog of open source books (Smith, 2012). Subsequently, the independent website Classroom Aid (n.d.) published an annotated list of sources for open source textbooks, many designed for college students (e.g., OpenStax College, College Open Textbook, Open Course Library, and Open Textbook

List). The community college instructional design team we interviewed hosted a speaker at their annual university professional development convocation who discussed open source materials. College leadership encouraged faculty members to maximize their use of open source materials to help defray students' textbook costs, which average 14% of tuition costs at 4-year public universities and 39% of tuition costs at community colleges, costs that cause students to jeopardize their grades by declining to buy assigned textbooks (Bidwell, 2014).

The Flipped Classroom.   The flipped classroom is an instructional strategy where students learn content at their own pace outside the classroom and subsequently participate in in-class, instructor-facilitated activities that apply, analyze, and/or evaluate this content. Flipped classroom activities include "interactive engagement, just-in-time teaching (in which students respond to web-based questions before class, and the professor uses this feedback to inform his or her teaching), and peer instruction" (Berrett, 2012, p. 1). The flipped classroom is a technological disruption with benefits: "The immediacy of teaching in this way enables students' misconceptions to be corrected well before they emerge on a midterm or final exam. The result, according to a growing body of research, is more learning" (p. 1). Students in flipped courses "showed gains at about twice the rate of those in traditional lectures at other institutions who took the same concept inventories" (p. 4).

But not everyone gives the flipped classroom an A+. Melissa E. Franklin, chair of Harvard University's physics department, reports that "the average score on a student evaluation of a flipped course is about half what the same professor gets when using the traditional lecture" (Berrett, 2012, p. 5). This is understandable, as students in flipped classrooms are expected to be active producers of educational products, content, commentary, and knowledge, and all learners are not equally enamored of this increased level of involvement and responsibility. Faculty roles are redefined by the flipped classroom as well. Franklin warns that faculty members need preparation to teach in flipped classrooms, including developing skill in answering student questions on the spot or reading students' questions right before class. She notes that few of her Harvard colleagues have adopted the flipped classroom: "For a normal, straight-ahead professor, there's a steep learning curve" (p. 5).

Technological Disruptions: Impact on Faculty

Massive open online courses (MOOCs) offer a worldwide audience free access to online course lectures, self-paced lessons, readings, problem sets, blogs, discussion boards, multiple choice and/or peer assessments, and sometimes online mentors and discussion group managers. MOOCs can reach massive audiences (as many as 300,000 at a time) with minimal outlay of faculty and institutional resources.

Students rate MOOCs positively: 63% of all course completers in a Massachusetts Institute of Technology electronics course described the course as better than an on-campus experience; 36% rated the course as comparable to an on-campus experience (Springer, 2013). However, fewer than 10% of students typically complete a MOOC (Allen, 2013).

According to one of our faculty interviewees who co-taught a MOOC at a large university, thousands of students enrolled. Many were traditional university students looking to engage in a nontraditional higher education online learning experience. Others were learners who would otherwise not have had the opportunity to take a university-level course. Participants new to higher education found the MOOC experience riveting, but expected more instructor attention to their discussion posts than was feasible or warranted by the MOOC delivery format. Our interviewee speculated that the MOOC functioned not as a university course but as an advertisement for introducing nontraditional learners to an entertaining, technologically enhanced experience.

Faculty members often view MOOCs as a negative disruption that threatens their connection with students and leaves them few meaningful roles in a digitized, outsourced higher education landscape. In 2012, Harvard professors expressed concerns about MOOCs causing diminished job prospects for faculty and graduate students, but in 2013, San Jose State University partnered with a MOOC provider to create a pilot program that clearly specified that faculty members would teach MOOC courses while the MOOC provider contributed platform support and student mentors (Fain, 2013). Concerns remain, however, that MOOCs represent one of many forms of outsourced digitized subject offerings that will displace online offerings created by local faculty experts.

Online Professional Development.   The community college design team we interviewed reported that their college requires online teaching faculty to complete a 6-week, 4-hours-per-week training course offered by the state online network. Faculty members must successfully complete this course to be eligible to teach online. Our university has developed a program called Faculty Development Online Learning Community (FDOLC) to engage faculty members in online course development and implementation. Faculty members teaching courses integral to the university's online instructional portfolio participate in a 14-week, 10-hours-per-week instructional program. Fully developed online courses are submitted for Quality Matters review and certification, an external monitoring system that emphasizes alignment and integration of course components such as learning objectives, assessment and measurement, instructional materials, course activities and learner interaction, and course technology to ensure quality learning outcomes (the Quality Matters Program Higher Education Program Rubric) (Quality Matters, 2014).

The FDOLC director outlined five primary responsibilities for online teaching faculty: (1) determining instructional content, (2) responding to no more than 10% of student discussion posts, (3) having online courses available for students 2 weeks prior to the class start date, (4) creating announcements and responding to student queries, and (5) assessing student work. She stated that while research indicates that adult online learners prefer asynchronous learning, faculty members who want synchronous student connections can accomplish them through online audio and video technologies.

Learning Object Repositories.   Learning object repositories (LORs) are digital collections of resources that are shared, reused, and/or modified by user groups (Edutech Wiki, n.d.; Metros & Bennett, 2002). Small-scale, single-purpose localized in-house LORs are highly useful in mentoring full-time and part-time faculty members who teach multiple sections of a course. One of the authors (Leon) has built an LOR housed on the university's LMS to mentor faculty members who teach multiple sections of an online and face-to-face survey course. The LOR provides asynchronous low-cost, efficient faculty mentoring plus high buy-in and participation via shared course planning, delivery, and joint construction of the LOR.

This LOR contains a dynamic array of strategies for meeting externally mandated compliance regulations of the Higher Learning Commission (an independent accrediting body for degree-granting postsecondary educational institutions in the North Central region of the United States), local institutional compliance regulations, sample course syllabi for varied course delivery formats, instructional materials, pedagogical strategies, assessment tools, supplemental resource articles and websites, and faculty discussion forums. Faculty members select, contribute, and modify LOR learning objects in ways that meet individual instructional needs and fulfill mandated compliance regulations. By maintaining an optimal balance between compliance and academic freedom, the LOR represents a beneficial technological disruption for faculty.

Technological Disruptions: Impact on Administrators

According to Dean S., "The political and public winds have changed against higher education. The value of college and degrees is being questioned. College is seen as an elitist institution that is unaware of the real world. There are efforts underway in Washington to change higher education significantly." These words succinctly capture the technological disruption facing college administrators today. Administrators are tasked with maintaining institutional financial solvency, which they accomplish by lending support to successful existing academic programs and services and by exploring and overseeing new academic ventures that have revenue-generating potential. Both activities rely on deliberative and judicious incorporation of technological innovation.

Administrators are also responsible for motivating faculty members by providing them with meaningful work. Today's administrators monitor and map faculty talent and time in order to allocate these resources economically and effectively to promote maximal faculty and student productivity and satisfaction. To address this need, faculty and administrators at some universities jointly craft a plan that enables faculty members with appropriate expertise (talent) to teach courses outside the academic departments that initially hired them.

Deliberative Responses to Innovation That Benefit Administrators. Today's faculty members are expected to scrupulously account for apportionment of load hours toward teaching, research, service, and governance. All courses taught must meet a prescribed number of seat hours or Carnegie units to ensure that students are receiving the instructional time promised by published, legally binding syllabi. In some institutions, faculty members are required to craft SMART goals (Meyer, 2003), goals that are *specific* (target a specific area for improvement), *measurable* (quantify or at least suggest an indicator of progress), *attainable* (how the goal can be accomplished), *realistic* (what results can realistically be achieved with available resources), and *tied to university goals* (advance institutional and professional mission). Faculty load and faculty goals are typically stored digitally to promote joint access and dynamic co-construction by faculty members and administrators to assure faculty talent is developed and mapped to align with institutional priorities and goals.

To comply with Higher Learning Commission standards and those mandated by other accrediting bodies, faculty members in some colleges and universities embed an accountability template into their syllabi that measures the number of direct (in-class) and indirect (out-of-class) instructional hours delivered by the course. Faculty members may also be required to state specific measurable outcomes in the course syllabus that are aligned with student evaluation of instruction tools. One such tool is Individual Development and Educational Assessment (IDEA), which enables students to evaluate instructors on specific course objectives. IDEA's mission is to provide assessment and feedback systems to improve learning in higher education. Faculty load, goals, and course hours as well as measurable course learning outcomes and assessments are being stored in electronic repositories. Faculty members regularly contribute to these repositories, which are accessed by both faculty members and administrators.

Administrators must prepare their institutions to meet external compliance requirements to assure fidelity and accountability of their online offerings. This includes monitoring fraud, an increasing priority of the federal government and a concern that can be partly assuaged via competency-based distance learning programs. Quality assurance of online course offerings and fidelity of delivery are issues of interest for both institutions of higher education and the federal government. Dean S. noted that adopting competency-based online programming moves the accountability needle "away from time spent learning and towards what students actually know." Submitting online courses to an outside reviewing agency such as

Quality Matters is another means for producing quality online courses and programs.

The Potential of Online Course and Program Offerings.   Allen and Seaman's (2013) 10-year longitudinal study on technological disruption in higher education provides fascinating insights regarding the growth of online education initiatives. They report that in 2002, fewer than half of colleges and university chief academic leaders considered online education critical to their long-term strategy. By 2012, this figure had jumped to 69%. To date, almost one third of all college students are currently taking at least one course in which at least 80% of course content is delivered online. Allen and Seaman (2013) further report that 77% of academic leaders rated learning outcomes in online education as the same as or superior to those in face-to-face classes.

Despite their popularity, online courses in higher education present challenges: 45% of academic leaders acknowledge that "it takes more faculty time and effort to teach online" (Allen & Seaman, 2013, p. 9), 89% believe students need more discipline to succeed in online courses, 90% report lower student retention rates to be an important or very important barrier to online learning ventures, and 40% worry about potential employers rejecting graduates' online degrees (Allen & Seaman, 2013). Additionally, challenges associated with faculty members' resistance to the adoption of online education were particularly acute. In 2012, only 30% of chief academic officers agreed with the statement "faculty at my school accept the value and legitimacy of online education" (p. 44). Over two thirds of chief academic officers felt that "lack of acceptance of online instruction by faculty as a barrier to the growth of online instruction" was important or very important (p. 44).

A key idea in designing and implementing online learning is that teaching online requires increased faculty time and effort. Thus, administrators must consider ways to provide faculty members with released time to develop new online courses and programs and learn best practices in online instructional pedagogy. These would include (but not be limited to) co-planning to develop curriculum, engage in course design, learn new technologies and use them to expand the curriculum, and (because student attrition is higher in online courses) scaffold the needs of all learners for maximum engagement and content/skill mastery. Administrators already must create marketing strategies that favorably position their college's or university's online curriculum offerings in an increasingly competitive market. Dean S. stated that his university networks with local television and newspapers to obtain free news coverage about its competency-based online program as well as leveraging social media to advertise programs.

Establishing online programs can be expensive. In an era of diminishing economic resources, higher education administrators must find ways of containing costs without sacrificing instructional quality. One way universities are approaching this issue is to form consortia. At present, the

NEW DIRECTIONS FOR HIGHER EDUCATION • DOI: 10.1002/he

Higher Learning Commission is forming a consortium consisting of Arizona University, Capella University, and the University of Wisconsin in an effort to develop the type of integrated competency-based distance education effort favored by the federal government, a pilot program projected to yield rich results.

In the book *Saving Higher Education*, Bradley, Seidman, and Painchaud (2011) speak of the need for greater flexibility and reduced seat hour time, reflecting many administrators' concerns about cost containment. Bradley et al. (at Southern New Hampshire University) suggest modularizing courses to reduce the 4-year university curriculum to 3 years. Our university has made a similar foray into modularization as a response to requests for the creation of strategic online course content. A number of online courses are being created that offer instructional modules within a single course that students can logically access in any sequence. This type of modularization provides definite benefits in project-based courses that require students to integrate large amounts of related material that is of coequal importance. At present, the university administration has assembled a group of in-house professionals that includes instructional designers. In an interview, the director of online operations described the purpose of the group as exploring viability and potential of blended learning and the learning theories that drive current blended learning practices. This group is using a community of inquiry framework to investigate the degree of success represented by ongoing blended course offerings and to provide insight into future directions in which blended learning initiatives could proceed.

Future Directions

Our analysis of technological disruption trends in higher education suggests that higher education will:

- Continue to see a rise in anytime, anywhere online delivery of instructional content to students that will encompass instructional strategies gleaned from MOOCs, the flipped classroom, and quality-managed localized online course development efforts.
- Utilize open source materials increasingly, especially those that have been peer reviewed, and that these open source materials will eventually replace textbooks in undergraduate introductory courses.
- Continue to have an uneasy relationship with outsourced online curriculum, which will motivate faculty members to actively engage in efforts to define a meaningful role for themselves within outsourced programs and in online teaching in general.
- Reap ongoing benefits for faculty members derived from online connection both with other scholars and with local university colleagues, although it is projected that faculty members will perceive losses in day-to-day face-to-face community interaction.

- Impel faculty members to continue searching for ways to remain relevant in their teaching role, including sustaining a personalized presence in online asynchronous instruction.
- Experience a proliferation of competency-based online programs, with multi-university consortiums being formed to consolidate intellectual and economic resources.

While the pace of technological disruption in higher education proceeds too fast for some and not fast enough for others, it is hoped that, like Yameel, technological disruption will continue to help colleges and universities deliver all that they have to offer expediently and effectively while preserving the heart and soul of their educational missions.

References

Allen, I. E., & Seaman, J. (2013). *Changing course: Ten years of tracking online education in the United States*. Babson Park, MA: Babson Survey Research Group and Quahog Research Group. Retrieved from http://www.onlinelearningsurvey.com/reports/changingcourse.pdf

Allen, J. (2013). The ABCs of MOOCs. *On Wisconsin, 114*(2), 28–31.

Berrett, D. (2012, February 19). How "flipping" the classroom can improve the traditional lecture. *Chronicle of Higher Education*. Retrieved from http://moodle.technion.ac.il/file.php/1298/Announce/How_Flipping_the_Classroom_Can_Improve_the_Traditional_Lecture.pdf

Bidwell, A. (2014, January 28). Report: High textbook prices have college students struggling. *U.S. News & World Report*. Retrieved from http://www.usnews.com/news/articles/2014/01/28/report-high-textbook-prices-have-college-students-struggling

Blin, F., & Munro, M. (2008). Why hasn't technology disrupted academics' teaching practices? Understanding resistance to change through the lens of activity theory. *Computers and Education, 50*(2), 475–490.

Bower, J. L., & Christensen, C. M. (1995, January–February). Disruptive technologies: Catching the wave. *Harvard Business Review*. Retrieved from http://hbr.org/1995/01/disruptive-technologies-catching-the-wave/

Bradley, M. J., Seidman, R. H., & Painchaud, S. R. (2011). *Saving higher education: The integrated, competency-based three-year bachelor's degree program*. San Francisco, CA: Jossey-Bass.

Carr, N. (2012, September 27). The crisis in higher education. *MIT Technology Review*. Retrieved from http://www.technologyreview.com/computing/41350/

Classroom Aid. (n.d.). *Open textbooks and materials for open source education*. Retrieved from http://classroom-aid.com/open-educational-resources/curriculum/

Edutech Wiki. (n.d.). Learning object repository. Retrieved from http://edutechwiki.unige.ch/en/Learning_object_repository

Fain, P. (2013, January 16). As California goes? *Inside Higher Ed*. Retrieved from http://www.insidehighered.com/news/2013/01/16/california-looks-moocs-online-push

Honeycutt, B., & Glova, S. (2014, March 31). Can you flip an online class? *Faculty Focus*. Retrieved from http://www.facultyfocus.com/

Metros, S. E., & Bennett, K. (2002). Learning objects in higher education. *EDUCAUSE Center for Applied Research: Research Bulletin, 2002*(19), 1–10.

Meyer, P. J. (2003). *Attitude is everything: If you want to succeed above and beyond*. Waco, TX: Meyer Resource Group.

Quality Matters. (2014). Retrieved from https://www.qualitymatters.org/

Rice University. (2014). OpenStax College. Retrieved from http://openstaxcollege.org/

Schwartz, D. I., & Hass, M. (2001). Be mystical. Be happy. In S. M. Matlins (Ed.), *The Jewish Lights spirituality handbook: A guide to understanding, exploring & living a spiritual life* (pp. 106–112). Woodstock, VT: Jewish Lights Publishing.

Smith, M. (2012, May 10). Textbook alternative. *Inside Higher Ed*. Retrieved from http://www.insidehighered.com/news/2012/05/10/university-minnesota-compiles-database-peer-reviewed-open-source-textbooks

Springer, R. (2013, July 5). MOOCs change playing field in higher education. Retrieved from https://www.indiawest.com/news/11906-moocs-change-playing-field-in-higher-education.html

Vai, M., & Sosulski, K. (2011). *Essentials of online course design: A standards-based guide.* New York: Routledge.

MARJORIE ROTH LEON, PhD, *is the director of curriculum development and an associate professor in the Educational Foundations and Inquiry program in the College of Education at National Louis University.*

TODD ALAN PRICE, PhD, *is the director of policy studies and program coordinator for Educational Foundations and Inquiry in the College of Education at National Louis University.*

NEW DIRECTIONS FOR HIGHER EDUCATION • DOI: 10.1002/he

INDEX